The importance of spotting elephants

Here is a refreshing book that every marketer must read. It tells us how quickly the science of marketing has fallen behind the times, and what we have to do to prevent the marketing elephant from turning into a dinosaur. Suman Srivastava writes with conviction, and he tells his wonderful stories with great passion. The ten interesting elephants which are featured in this book are captivating, they provoke us, they reveal the traps we must avoid, and eventually they leave us with excellent insights into how we can become very effective marketers.

Harish Bhat
Author of 'Tata Log'
Member, Group Executive Council, Tata Sons

Marketing Unplugged is a joy to read ... and is a wake up call! The book is a remarkable balance of observation, insight, relevance, and challenge. And it does that all (thanks to the Elephant in the room) with a real sense of wit and humour ...Suman makes a powerful argument that traditional marketing strategy is simply not equipped to deal with the reality of today's reality. It is convincing that new and fresh and innovative techniques are not only needed ...they are mandatory. And you will love getting to know the elephant!

Bob Schmetterer
Former Chairman and CEO, Euro RSCG Worldwide
Author of 'Leap! A Revolution in Creative Business Strategy'

Marketing Unplugged is an interesting blend of wisdom, experience and insights, distilled by a master craftsman into an easy-to-use toolkit and garnished with real brand stories. Suman calls out the elephants in the room and shows you how the old rules of marketing have become irrelevant. A fun read. Totally unputdownable.

Prakash Iyer
Former Managing Director of Kimberly-Clark Lever,
Author of 'The habit of winning' & 'The secret of leadership'

The world of marketing is changing fast. Keeping up with all the changes is hard. In this book, Suman has done an amazing job of distilling the lessons of the new world of marketing into a coherent narrative. He has done this in an entertaining and lucid manner with examples from India and abroad. His discourse isn't limited to marketing alone and he talks of history, politics, religion and sports along the way. A must read for all young marketing professionals.

Chander Sethi
Chairman & Managing Director, South East Asia, Reckitt Benckiser

MARKETING UNPLUGGED

Spotting the Elephants in the Room

Suman Srivastava

CINNAMONTEAL
PUBLISHING

First published in India in 2016 by CinnamonTeal Publishing

Copyright © 2016 Suman Srivastava

ISBN 978–93–85523–50–2

Typesetting: CinnamonTeal Publishing

Cover illustration and book illustrations: Gynelle Alves
Idea for illustrations: Rachna Dhall-Haasnoot.

CinnamonTeal Publishing
an imprint of Dogears Print Media Pvt. Ltd.
Plot No 16, Housing Board Colony
Gogol, Margao
Goa 403601 India
www.cinnamonteal.in

CONTENTS

From the Elephant in the Room

Hello.

I am the elephant in the room. You know that phrase, of course. It means an obvious truth that is ignored or not acknowledged.

I am used to being ignored. Lots of very smart people use very smart arguments to avoid having to deal with me. I find it very funny. Why are they so shy of me?

But let me explain what I am doing here. This guy, Suman, has written this book that you are about to read. He claims that his task is to spot the elephants in the room and help others spot them too. Basically, he is turning the spotlight on to me.

Suman is trying to say that marketers have these pet theories and they cling on to them even though they may be wrong. He has identified ten of these theories - ten elephants in the room as he calls them - which he tries to debunk.

Well, I don't like this spotlight on me. Here I have been sitting comfortably in the room, not being disturbed by anyone, watching with amusement as marketers try to step gingerly around me. And now, Suman is trying to get me out of here.

So, I have a plan. I am going to make fun of Suman. I am going to argue that he is wrong and there is nothing wrong with the elephants in the room. It will be fun to see who wins.

Enjoy the book. Suman has written all the boring, serious stuff with case studies and things. I appear only in the fun, cartoony stuff. We are on opposite sides of each issue. It is up to you to decide who is right.

Vote for me, though. OK?

THE REASON FOR THIS BOOK

The Technology of Marketing

My wife, Jasmeet, agreed to visit the Mercedes Benz museum in Stuttgart, Germany, only because our son and I were so insistent. But by the time we ended the tour of the museum, Jasmeet was almost converted to the automobile religion. Indeed, it is hard to treat cars merely as a means of transport after you have heard of the exploits of the truly devout saints of the automobile faith.

As we walked across various levels of the museum, we were struck by the dramatic changes in car technology that have taken place in every decade since its evolution. Each decade not only had its own fashion in terms of looks, but also new advances in engineering and technology. New innovations get introduced in high-end cars, but within a decade or two, they become the norm for all cars.

I bought my first car twenty years ago. It was an almost new Premier Padmini that I loved with the passion reserved for a 'first' anything. The Premier Padmini had a carburetor at the heart of the engine and car owners of that era needed to be auto-cardiologists to ensure this heart kept going perfectly.

Today, my car does not have a carburetor. Most modern cars come with an electronic fuel injection (EFI) system that is so different from the old system that my bag of tricks for managing a temperamental carburetor is now totally redundant. The new fuel injection system is more efficient, uses less fuel and throws far fewer tantrums. Ah, the wonders of technological progress.

Every industry has its own version of the 'carburetor – EFI' story, except marketing. Marketing tends to get stuck in the old way of doing things and hates change. It is as if an automobile saint has decreed that all cars will have a carburetor forever and ever. Amen.

Maybe this is because marketing doesn't use hard technology, but ideas and principles, which tend to be sticky. The great economic historian, Karl Marx, had noticed this stickiness and written about it at the end of the 19th century. He called hard technology the means of production. Around these means of production were a set of ideas and beliefs that he called the 'social superstructure'. He found that when the means of production changed, the social superstructure needed to change too, but did so only with a lag. Often, such change required a violent revolution.

Maybe, that is the state that marketing is in currently. Marketing developed its core technologies in the sixties and has been using the same technology ever since. New ideas have been developed and written about, but not incorporated into mainstream marketing. It is as if the R&D division is coming up with innovations, but the factory managers are refusing to incorporate them into the cars they are building.

That is what this book is about: an attempt to point out the elephants in the room of marketers. The obvious truths that we tend to ignore either because it is too hard to recognise the truth or because we are used to working in the old fashion.

This book will highlight the flaws in the old way of thinking. It will also highlight a new line of thought that already exists but is not being used on a day to day basis. This new thought stream is not my own, but has been written about by academicians and evolved practitioners. My role here is to compile into a coherent story, the advances that have been made in the area of marketing thinking since the turn of the century.

The book is an organisation of commonly held beliefs that have become elephants in the room. Around each belief is a series of short articles highlighting an argument or an example to show that the belief is either wrong or only partially correct or, at the very least, has another side to it.

This book is not trying to become a manual for the new marketing paradigm. It only aims to create debate and discussion among marketing practitioners and nudge them into questioning some of the basic beliefs that they hold.

If you believe that technology needs to evolve or die, if you wonder whether the concept of branding is dead or dying, if you believe that marketing is a function that deserves serious respect or if you get frustrated by the lack of innovation in the marketing function; then this book is for you.

First, let me tell you exactly how old this marketing technology is.

Would you Build a Car Using Sixties Technology?

The sixties sound like such a long time ago - five decades ago, half a century ago, or fifty years ago. Indeed, a long time back. There is no industry that still uses the technology that was invented so long ago. Can you imagine driving a car invented in that era? We have given up on the Ambassador and the Premier Padmini even in India. How about going to a doctor who hasn't updated his knowledge since the sixties?

Well, there is one field of specialisation that still uses technology invented in the sixties or earlier. That field is marketing.

There are people who still talk about the Unique Selling Proposition or the USP, a concept invented in the 1940s by an employee of Ted Bates & Company, Rosser Reeves.

We still use the AIDA model to understand consumer behaviour. AIDA stands for Awareness, Interest, Desire and Action and attempts to explain the various stages through which a consumer passes before he or she makes a brand choice. This model was invented in the year 1898 by a man with the colourful name of E. St. Elmo Lewis. Yes, you read it right; it was in the nineteenth century! Mr. Elmo Lewis was an insurance salesman and invented the concept to help train others to sell life insurance. He would not be out of place in today's world.

Professor Neil Borden of Harvard Business School introduced the concept of Marketing Mix to the world in the year 1953. At that time, he was building on the ideas of his colleague, James Culliton, who had first compared marketing to cooking in the year 1948. The ingredients that went into the Marketing Mix then are the same even now.

Professor E. Jerome McCarthy of Michigan State University came up with the idea of 4Ps in the year 1960. Some people have attempted to add a P or two more to the original concept, but the idea is still very much the foundation of marketing thought all over the world.

No discussion in marketing ever takes place without the word Positioning coming up. This was an idea first proposed by Jack Trout in June 1969 in an article that he wrote in the *Industrial Marketing* magazine. In the year 1981, along with Al Reis, he wrote a book called *Positioning* that became a global best seller. The year 1981 sounds quite recent, but please remember that it was 30+ years ago.

Marketing strategy really came of age when Stanley Pollitt invented the concept of account planning in advertising agencies. Mr. Pollitt felt that marketing decisions were being made with inadequate data and insufficient thought and invented a research-based process that improved the quality of marketing strategy. When did he invent this? In the year 1965!

Many of the ideas and processes that Mr. Pollitt and his contemporary, Stephen King (not the novelist but the planner at J. Walter Thompson, who is considered by some as the father of account planning), used in the 1960s are still in vogue today.

Marketing strategy uses research and one of the most important research techniques in use today is the focus group discussion (FGD). This technique was invented by an American sociologist named Robert King Merton who first conducted an FGD in the year 1941. He subsequently published a book on the usage of this technique in the year 1946. Mr. Merton's ideas were used and glorified by Ernest Dichter who is considered to be the father of motivational research. Dr. Dichter was the first person to apply Freudian principles of psychoanalysis to marketing, inventing psychographic segmentation and everything that goes with it. Dr. Dichter did most of his work in the forties and the fifties. His methods find prominent mention in the 1957 book, *The Hidden Persuaders*, by Vance Pickard.

I could go on, but I think you get the idea.

The question now is this: Are all these old ideas still valid?

These were ideas and tools that were created for a different era. An era where consumers were more innocent of the tricks of marketers and advertisers, an era when there was no internet or social media, an era when mass media was really mass and dominant, an era where brands had power over retailers and not the other way around. Moreover, these ideas were created to market mostly packaged goods.

I need hardly remind you that the world has changed dramatically since the 1960s. How can we still be using the ideas and tools of the 1960s to solve the problems of the 2010s? It is not as if there aren't any new ideas around. Several books and articles have been written about new ways of marketing (some of these books are discussed in the pages to follow). The problem is that, as marketers, we are so comfortable with the old way of working that we don't want to adopt any new ideas.

There is a lot of talk these days about revolutions and second independence movements. Well, marketing needs a revolution too; the old ideas must be thrown out and new ones ushered in.

ELEPHANT IN THE ROOM:

MARKETING IS NOT A SCIENCE

If Physics can't, can Marketing?

Human beings have always hated surprises. Mankind has worked hard to understand the laws of nature to predict what would happen next. We have built up fanciful theories about the stars, the lines on our palms and even tea leaves to predict what fate is likely to befall us in the future.

A lot of science is also driven by the same desire. Isaac Newton discovered the law of gravity; other scientists built on that. By the beginning of the 20th century, with many advances in the field of science, many physicists thought the end of Physics was near. They believed that we had only a few remaining puzzles to solve before arriving at the deterministic model of the universe. This was meant to be the model that could fully explain the future of the world if we could know the starting values of a set of variables.

Then Werner Heisenberg came up with the Uncertainty Principle.

The Uncertainty Principle says that we can either know the velocity or the position of a particle, never both. This was big news in the world of Physics. It created a huge uproar and even as eminent a scientist as Albert Einstein famously said, "I don't believe God plays dice with the universe." Well, that wasn't exactly what he said. He had written a long critique of the Uncertainty Principle and had ended up saying, "I, at any rate, am convinced that 'He' does not throw dice." But the other construction stuck, as it sounded much cooler.

Over time, the Uncertainty Principle became accepted and even Einstein bowed to its logic. This time he gave a more favourable statement: "I have second thoughts. Maybe God is malicious."

Once they accepted that we live in an uncertain world, Physicists went on to properly understand the structure of the atom. This understanding directly led to all the most important inventions of the last century – computers, plastics, nuclear power and space travel.

Physics embraced uncertainty a century ago and moved on to great things. But the business and marketing worlds are only just waking up to this reality.

It sounds quite bizarre that an exact science like Physics gave up on certainty a century ago, while an inexact science like marketing still lives with the opposite belief.

Coming back to marketing, it seems that marketing desperately wants to become a science. It is like a teenager who acts like a grown-up. It puts on airs, speaks in strange accents and tries to pretend that it likes the taste of alcohol.

Everyone else smiles indulgently, except when they get irritated.

Marketing believes that everyone will give it respect if marketing could predict the future accurately. Marketers think that chefs get more respect than them because chefs can mix a set of ingredients in a certain way and get the same result each time they do so. Marketers, on the other hand, have to cross their fingers, pray to all they hold sacred and hold their breaths to see the consequences of their actions.

Is that a bad thing? I don't think so. There are a lot of professions that cannot predict the outcome in advance on the basis of the input provided. Take music for instance; it doesn't matter how many times the group has rehearsed or performed together, no two shows are exactly the same. It may be due to the musicians' mood, the crowd or the acoustics in the hall. Whatever the reasons, the results are never the same.

And we love it.

Today, marketing has been taken over by quants. Quants, or quantitatively oriented people, who think it's only a matter of time before all their tools are sharp to a point where they can accurately predict the future.

The world of market research is full of fancy models. Models that help marketers test every aspect of their marketing mix and then test the whole package altogether. Even the language of market research sounds a lot like that of Physics at the beginning of the last century. We, the marketers, talk of quantitative modelling and independent variables. We do regression analysis and multi-variate ones at that. We hope to create a deterministic model of the universe.

Nothing wrong with that except the best marketing ideas never developed in this way. The biggest ideas in Physics have been dreamt up by guys scribbling on blackboards. In the case of marketing, the scribbling often happens on paper napkins, but the outcome is the same. It is the incremental improvements that come from the fancy models. The big ideas seem to come from nowhere.

Apple doesn't seem to believe a lot in market research. The success of Starbucks could not have been predicted by research, nor that of Google, Facebook or Nirma. The success of Pan Parag probably surprised even its founders. Most great marketers talk about luck. They talk about intuition, gut feel and instinct. I have not heard anyone attribute their success to conjoint analysis.

I am not being mean to quants. You see, I have been one of them. I have been seduced by the sexiness of hard data. I actually know how conjoint analysis is done and have talked at length about the merits and demerits of factor analysis.

I have also been a quali type - one of those touchy, feely planners who believe only in projective techniques to understand the psyche of consumers. Indeed, my wife is a qualitative researcher, and my family budget owes a lot to the popularity of focus groups.

In other words, I have also been a laptop carrying member of the MBA tribe and presented papers at market research forums like ESOMAR (the international association of market researchers). I don't hate the tools; just that I am worried about the over reliance on them and the mindless way that some marketers tend to use them.

The problem is that these marketers have fled the responsibility of decision making by hiding behind the sandbags of market research.

I will return to the subject of market research later. For now let's learn from a guru who explains why quants get things so wrong. You will see several 'Guru-speak' sections in this book. Each of them is a synopsis of a book which is relevant to the subject we are talking about. Over to the first Guru-speak.

Guru-speak: Black Swan

Nassim Nicholas Taleb is the prosecutor-in-chief at the inquisition of the quants. He is much in demand these days as everyone is concerned about the collapse of the financial markets in the year 2008 and the lessons it has to teach us.

The quants are being blamed for nearly destroying the world's financial markets. MBA has become a particularly bad word because of this reason. Wall Street has moved rapidly from being the dream destination for the brightest youth of the world to being treated like a part of the red light district; attractive, but not a place to be openly visiting.

Mr. Taleb's central point is that, just like sex, the tendency to get seduced by techniques that bring order in our lives is natural and built into human nature. He seems to regard it as yet another vice. He raves against it, quite like a pastor would rave against drinking. He has written several books on the subject, *Black Swan* being the most famous one.

The name comes from the fact that until the year 1697, nobody in the Northern Hemisphere had ever seen a black swan. So, everyone believed that all swans are white. In fact, swans were characterised by their white colour back then. Then, in the year 1697, some explorers discovered black swans in Australia and that upset the entire theory of swans being white. Up until the discovery of black swans, there was no way in which anyone could have predicted their existence. However, their existence caused major disruption to the original theory.

Nassim Taleb has defined *Black Swan* events as having three major characteristics. The first is that they are extremely rare, leading us to believe that they don't really exist. The second is that they have extreme impact. And the third is that they have retrospective (but not prospective) predictability. In other words, you cannot predict their occurrence before they happen, but they seem obvious afterwards.

The financial collapse of the year 2008 had all these characteristics. The event was obviously very rare - the last one had taken place in the year 1929. The impact of the crash was so massive that perhaps we still haven't seen all the changes that it is likely to create. In spite of all the sophisticated models developed by the brightest minds on the planet, the financial system was not able to predict the crash. Though, in retrospect, it seems obvious to even the least sophisticated politician.

The oil spill in the Gulf of Mexico from the oil rig owned by BP is another example of a Black Swan event. So is the impact on airlines of the eruption of the Icelandic volcano, Eyjafjallajokull. The author Paulo Coelho said in a tweet on April 18, 2010: "If 5 days ago, I had a new book on how a volcano in Iceland paralizes Europe, ppl would say 'Crazy, nonsense rubbish' "

The book, *Black Swan*, is really about the inability of the human brain to deal with extreme events, and our love for the normal. Mr. Taleb has a colourful way of explaining this to us.

Imagine, he says, there is a stadium full of people. We measure the height of all the people in the stadium and work out the average. Now, we bring into the stadium the tallest person in the world. What would happen to the average? Nothing much. One outlier observation is not going to make much of a difference to the average. We can practically ignore the existence of that extreme observation. This is the world of Mediocristan.

Now imagine that instead of recording the heights of the people in the stadium, we record their wealth and work out the average. As before, we bring into the stadium another person after taking out the average. Only this time, he would be the richest person in the world. We will now see that the average changes drastically. In fact, the average will change so dramatically that all our previous data would become totally inconsequential. This one outlier observation would change everything. This is the world of Extremistan.

We all believe that we live in Mediocristan, when we actually live in Extremistan. And therein lies the problem.

Extremistan is a place where wild, random events occur. You cannot predict what will happen next. All the data that you collect about past occurrences does nothing to prepare you for the next one. There is no native in this group - each new individual seems to belong to a different species. The conditions of the group are determined by just a few members, and history moves with big jumps. It is usually hard to figure out what is going on, but when something does happen, it changes everything in a dramatic fashion. This is a world where the winner takes it all.

Mediocristan is a place where there is only mild randomness. The typical member is mediocre and the more information that you have about the current members, the lesser you are surprised by every new one. Observation actually leads to knowledge that leads to predictability. The winners take only a small share of the cake. The masses win here rather than the individual. The future is easy to predict and here history crawls along without any sudden jerks or jumps.

You see, Extremistan is not a very nice place. Yes, there are elements of it that are attractive to our wild side, but really, Extremistan is not a girl you can bring home to your parents. Mediocristan, on the other hand, is just right. Nice, stable, moderate - the perfect world to live in.

Why do we like living in Mediocristan so much? Taleb suggests that it is because we prefer certainty to uncertainty and because we like to learn the precise over the general. We like the known and the repeated. These two factors combine to form an elegant analytical tool called the Bell Curve, which Taleb labels as the Great Intellectual Fraud.

The bell curve postulates that most things in life follow a normal distribution (there is that word again!). In other words, most observations of the event would cluster around the arithmetic mean and very few of them would occur in the areas of the two tails of the curve. The bell curve also puts a very precise value on how many observations are likely to occur in the middle of the curve and how many at the extremes. Since the values at the extremes are so rare, we are taught that it is safe to ignore them and focus on the middle.

Now we can see why experts think they can predict the future. The assumption is that the world operates according to the bell curve. This means that the more data you collect, the more robust and predictive your model would be.

We are taught to think of the normal and ignore the extremes. It is easier to think of the normal everyday events than to think of the bizarre events that change the course of history. We can't deal with the latter, except in retrospect.

The idea that Black Swans make sense only in retrospect is an interesting one and is the basis of all creativity.

Edward de Bono, the guru of creative thinking tools, says that the mind gets conditioned on how to move from point A to point B. So much so that it doesn't notice any detours along the way. This means that it cannot find a way to point C, which lies along one of the detours. However, if somehow you get to point C, then it is obvious how to reach point A from there. All creative thinking techniques try to interrupt our patterned thinking and try to make us think in new ways. In other words, try to get us to point C, from where we can get back to point A.

You need to be quite a creative person to be able to break out of patterns established in Mediocristan. You need imagination. Nassim Taleb says that most of us don't have imagination and we try to suppress it in others. We need to change our thinking and make extraordinary events the starting point to learn how to work with them rather than ignore them.

With the benefit of the insights that Mr. Taleb has given us, we can think of brilliant marketing as something that would create a Black Swan event for an industry that believes it is living in Mediocristan. We will discuss several Black Swan events in this book. Many stable industries have been disrupted by individuals, leading to changed market behaviour. However, the new market again settles down and waits for the next Black Swan.

If Marketing were a Science

In April 1985, the world realised that marketing was not a science.

On April 21, 1985, The Coca Cola Company replaced its main brand with a new one called New Coke. This was a new product with a different formulation - sweeter than the original. There was a huge uproar and the consumers hated the new brand. So much was the uproar that the company had to bring back the original formulation as Coca Cola Classic within three months of launching New Coke, which they had to withdraw.

For people of my generation, this is a well known story, almost a fable that we learnt about on our first marketing professor's knee. But I have discovered, to my surprise, that younger audiences have never heard of this story. Clearly, The Coca Cola Company and the marketing world have done a good job of hushing up this disaster story. This story is an important landmark on the journey to understanding why marketing is not a science and deserves a repetition here.

Coca Cola has always been the leader in the cola category. In the fifties, it had two thirds of the market, but by the year 1983, this share was down to around a quarter.

One of the reasons for this decline was the Pepsi taste test challenge. This started off as a tactical exercise where consumers were offered Coke and Pepsi in unbranded glasses and people were asked to choose the one they liked better. Most people liked Pepsi in these blind tests. Pepsi made films of these tests and ran them on TV.

Soon this challenge moved up from being a tactical exercise to becoming the core marketing message of Pepsi. The taste test blended well with Pepsi's brand thought, "The choice of a new generation."

This started to hurt Coca Cola and their market share started to decline. This led them to reformulate their product and launch it as New Coke.

Consumers were negative about this strategy from day one. Consumers said they hated the new drink and wanted the old one back. Thousands of phone calls and letters poured in. Media took up the cry. It was an absolute disaster. Within three months, the company realised that it had made a mistake and it brought back the original drink as Coca Cola Classic. For a short while, it sold the New Coke along side the Classic version, but soon New Coke was totally abandoned.

Pepsi was delighted with this whole mess that Coke got itself into. Pepsi helped stoke consumer and media opinion against the launch of New Coke. It proclaimed its victory in the cola war with full page ads in major newspapers - the ad was a congratulatory letter from Roger Enrico to all staff and bottlers of Pepsi. Later, Mr. Enrico wrote a book about this victory titled *The other guy blinked*.

What is amazing about this story is the fact that The Coca Cola Company is one of the world's most professional marketing companies. The launch of New Coke was the most important marketing move that they had ever made. They had huge research budgets and hired the best talent in the market. So how did they get the whole thing so wrong?

Before the launch, the CEO of The Coca Cola Company, Roberto Goizueta, exuded total confidence. In a press conference to announce the launch, he said, "The best has been made even better." He went on to say, "Some may choose to call this the boldest single marketing move in the history of the packaged-goods business, we simply call it the surest move ever made."

What conclusion do you draw when the 'surest move ever made' in marketing turned out to be a dud?

This is not the only example of a top notch marketing company making a big mistake. These examples are depressingly common.

A more recent disaster was the one around the logo of the retailer Gap. The company that owns this brand is called Gap Inc. and is a respected name in the retail business. Other than Gap, it also owns brands like Banana Republic, Old Navy, Piperlime, Athlete and Intermix. You could say that it is one of the marketing geniuses of the fashion industry.

And this marketing genius received such negative feedback from consumers when it changed its logo that it had to revert back to its old logo within a week.

The President of Gap, North America, wrote in her blog: "We want our customers to take notice of Gap and see what it stands for today. We chose this design as it's more contemporary and current. It honours our heritage through the blue box while still taking it forward."

I don't know how much it cost Gap to make the change twice over, but its share price fell by 13% and sales were down by 2% in that month.

So a major marketing move that was meant to modernise the brand and take it forward, resulted in a decrease in sales.

If you Google 'marketing disasters' you will find several others by large companies. Pepsi discovered that its slogan 'Pepsi brings you back to life' got translated into Chinese as 'Pepsi brings your ancestors back from the grave.' Even worse was the campaign launched by the Swedish company, Electrolux, for its vacuum cleaners in the USA, 'Nothing sucks like an Electrolux.'

Why did professional marketing companies like Coke, Gap, Pepsi and Electrolux make such mistakes? Didn't they do research? Couldn't they understand their consumers well enough? Aren't they the masters of communication? So what happened?

Well, what happened was that hubris got in the way. Marketing is not a science, though marketers like to pretend that it is. Scientists form hypothesis, they do research and they do rigorous statistical analysis. They also believe their results will always replicate in the real world. Unfortunately, consumers are human beings and they act in unpredictable and irrational ways. That causes all the problems.

Since consumers act in irrational ways, marketers who try to be too rational, tend to fail. Let me illustrate this with a story.

The 'Lever' isation of Marketing in India

In the year 1989, I was assigned to the team working on the Surf account in the advertising agency Lintas. Thus, I became one of the foot soldiers in the famous Indian detergent war. The detergent war is the story of a small Indian entrepreneur who caught the giant Hindustan Lever napping and how the giant hit back. This story helps us understand the relative strengths and weaknesses of entrepreneurs and giant corporations. And thus, is a case worth studying.

The war had started in the year 1969, when a man named Karsanbhai Patel started manufacturing a yellow detergent powder in a small shed and selling it on his bicycle. Right through the seventies, Mr. Patel grew his business by adding more manufacturing units, building up a sales force and strengthening his brand, Nirma.

At this time, Hindustan Lever did not notice this upstart competitor. There was no reason to. Nirma was a coarse product with low level of active detergent (the ingredient that actually does the cleaning), poor perfume and a tendency to make your hands burn when you mixed it in water. Surf, on the other hand, was an established sophisticated product that had active detergent level three times that of Nirma. Plus, it had a whitening agent and a fragrance that Indian consumers had learnt to love over the previous two decades. It was packed in a premium carton with smart graphics that was clearly superior to the screen printed plastic bag of Nirma. Finally, Hindustan Lever also had the support of retailers who were dependent on the company for a large part of their income. Therefore, Levers could bully the retailers into doing its bidding. It seemed like an unequal fight.

The main thing in favour of Nirma was the price. It was priced originally at one fifth the price of Surf, though that ratio had changed to one third by the time I came to work on Surf. The second thing in its favour was luck. Commercial television came to India in the early eighties and helped build Nirma into a brand that consumers loved. Most of us who watched TV in that era still have the Nirma jingle playing in our heads.

Nirma overtook Surf in the market in the year 1979 as the graph below shows. That's when Hindustan Lever woke up to this threat!

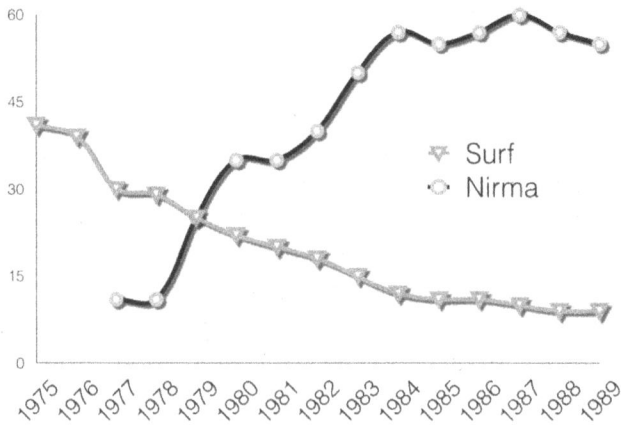

The rest of the story of the detergent war has been often told, so I will speed through it. Hindustan Lever was unable to contain Nirma through the first half of the eighties, though it tried hard. Surf focused on proving that it was twice as good as Nirma. Consumers accepted that claim, but Surf was three times the price of Nirma, so Nirma was still better value for money.

Eventually, the team at Lintas invented the hard nosed value seeking housewife, Lalitaji. Lalitaji was able to get through to Indian housewives with the message that Surf gave them a package of benefits that made it good value. It made the clothes last longer and made them whiter and brighter. Finally, the gap in the market share of the two detergents started to drop.

Hindustan Lever also introduced Wheel to fight Nirma at the same price point. Wheel attacked Nirma on the platform of safety to hands. Most consumers felt a tingling sensation when they mixed Nirma in water. A few reported rashes and other skin issues. Wheel made a big deal of this complaint and positioned itself as the safer detergent powder.

The combination of Lalitaji and Wheel ensured that Lever once again took the lead in market share over Nirma. It also ensured that Levers changed the way it approached the Indian market. Major changes were made in the production system, the distribution system and other aspects of the business. Hindustan Lever came through this war without the flab of the earlier years.

This marketing war illustrates the difference between challengers and professional marketers. The difference between entrepreneurs and giant corporations.

Nirma was an innovation that caused the detergent market in India to grow *fifteen* times in volume. Millions of women, who had never used a detergent powder before, were now able to do so. These women were saved from the hard labour of using a detergent cake to wash their clothes. Even Hindustan Lever benefitted from this. While the market share of Surf fell from around 40% to 9%, its volume actually doubled in the same period.

Only an entrepreneur could have introduced such a disruptive innovation. Large corporations fear this change because it endangers their leadership position.

Hindustan Lever's response is a classic case of a 'fast follower'. They entered the market for discount detergent powders late, but having done so, Levers produced a better product and marketed it better too. This is why that company is known to be such a great marketing company.

An executive coach, trainer and blogger called Stephen Remedios wrote: "Unilever has given over 500 CEOs to corporates across the world." I have no idea how he arrived at that number, but I would certainly agree that at least 500 companies in India have been influenced by the Lever way of thinking in marketing.

On the other hand, I do not know of even one company that has a CEO who had worked in Nirma during those heady years in the eighties. Though many entrepreneurs must have been inspired by this story, only a handful have gone on to successfully challenge other large corporations.

The moral of the story here is that the world needs both innovators and professional managers. Innovators do a great job in creating a market, while professionals create steady growth.

In the era immediately following the economic reforms in India, many new product categories in the technology, telecom & retail spaces were created and several of those companies were led by people from Hindustan Unilever. Many of these leaders failed, as they were unable to create the kind of disruptive innovations that were needed to succeed in the market. Later, as markets matured, Lever leaders gradually came into their own and now run these same companies in a professional way.

However, more innovations are needed to truly transform India into a developed country. Many of these innovations are related to production and product design. But many are required in marketing too. We need more Nirmas and fewer companies that have been 'Lever'ised.

I now want to return to the subject of market research and focus on why it often doesn't work.

The Problem with Research

If Venus had a moon, we would have been more environment friendly.

Isaac Asimov wrote a brilliant essay, *The Tragedy of the Moon*, to argue the above point. Beyond just arguing the point, Asimov's essay explains lucidly how science evolves on the basis of observations. And how it might have evolved if we had slightly different observations.

Two thousand years ago, mankind observed that the sun and the moon rise and set. Hence, the geocentric theory of the universe was evolved that said that the heavens revolved around the earth in set patterns. Initially, we thought that the sky was unmoving with the stars also fixed in it. Later we discovered that some stars (the planets) moved across the sky relative to the fixed stars. Not only did these stars move, they moved at times in one direction and, at other times, in the opposite direction.

This posed a bit of a problem for our theory, but we soon got around it and built some interesting and plausible theories to explain why all this was happening. Greek philosophers built a model of the universe with the earth at the center with fifty-six concentric spheres around it. Each sphere had one or more heavenly body in it and rotated around the earth in different patterns and speeds. The closest one contained the moon, the next contained the sun, the third Venus and so on.

There were alternative theories too. Two thousand five hundred years ago, there were Greek philosophers who had proposed a sun-centric view of the universe. However, this model did not explain the movements of the moon and, moreover, it said that the earth moved around the sun. This sounded illogical since the earth looked so massive, solid and immovable. So, this theory died and mankind went with the earth centric model.

Thinking about it, if the earth was at the center of the universe and human beings were the most important species on Earth, then it followed that the whole universe was really built with man at the center. As Asimov said:

"It is the earth that counts and only the earth. And on earth, only mankind counts. And of men, only one's country, one's city, one's tribe, one's family, one's self counts. The average person is geocentric, anthropocentric, ethnocentric and egocentric."

And so we evolved into the selfish creatures that we are, hell bent on destroying the earth and our eco-system due to our own egos.

But what if we didn't have a moon and instead Venus had one?

Then the brightest object in our night sky would not have been the moon, but Venus. And this beautiful, bright star would have spent six months of the year as the evening star visible for a few hours after the sun had set; and the other six months as the morning star, visible for a few hours before the sun rose. The morning and the evening stars had been observed two thousand five hundred years ago, but nobody thought that the two were the same. Now, if Venus had a moon that revolved around it, mankind would have surely made the connection between the morning and the evening stars. The only way to explain why one star rises in the morning for half the year and in the evening for the other half is that it revolves around the sun and its moon revolves around it.

Once we would have reached that conclusion, it would have been obvious that Mercury, Earth, Mars, Jupiter and Saturn also revolve around the sun and we would have arrived at the correct model of the universe, perhaps two thousand years before we finally did. On realising that we are just one planet in a solar system, we would have been forced to drop our geocentric, anthropocentric and egocentric view of life. Then, perhaps, we would have appreciated nature a bit more and not been as environmentally unsound as we are today.

That's how science works. By observing and building theories around those observations. It is only when a new observation comes along that doesn't fit our theory that we change our theory and move on.

If marketing is a science, it too should learn by observation. That sounds like a simple and obvious statement but marketers don't observe much. We prefer to go and ask questions from our consumers rather than just hide and observe what they are doing.

Children lie. Even when they get caught red handed with jam all over their face, they try to deny it. Loveable liars.

And when they grow up, they never really stop lying, especially to market researchers. They smoke and claim not to. They don't reveal their real income. They tell researchers what they think they should tell, rather than the reality.

"The trouble with market research is that people don't think how they feel, they don't say what they think, and they don't do what they say," said David Ogilvy

The best way to study children is by observing them at play, at school and at home. That's how psychologists arrive at their diagnosis. The best way to understand consumers is also by observing them in the act.

And the best time to observe consumers is when they are in a store. Retailers know consumers better than marketers who don't go into the field much. They get to see the consumers in the actual process of buying. Retailers know whether or not the consumers read the labels, which products get compared most with each other, and which promotions work better.

One of the pioneers of retail observation research is Paco Underhill. His firm has been in the consumer observation business for several years and he has written a book about his findings especially with regard to the American consumer. It's called, *Why We Buy: The Science of Shopping.* Sixteen years after the book was published, it is still not widely understood in the marketing community. We still ask consumers rather than observe them. So much for marketing being a science!

ELEPHANT IN THE ROOM:

MARKETING IS NOT WAR

BUT SUMAN, MARKETING IS WAR!
YOU HAVE TO FIGHT TO WIN! I AM AN ALPHA MALE!
THE COMPETITION RUNS FROM ME! SEE MY TUSKS!
FEEL MY KICKS AND CHOPS! HEAR MY HAI-YAAS...

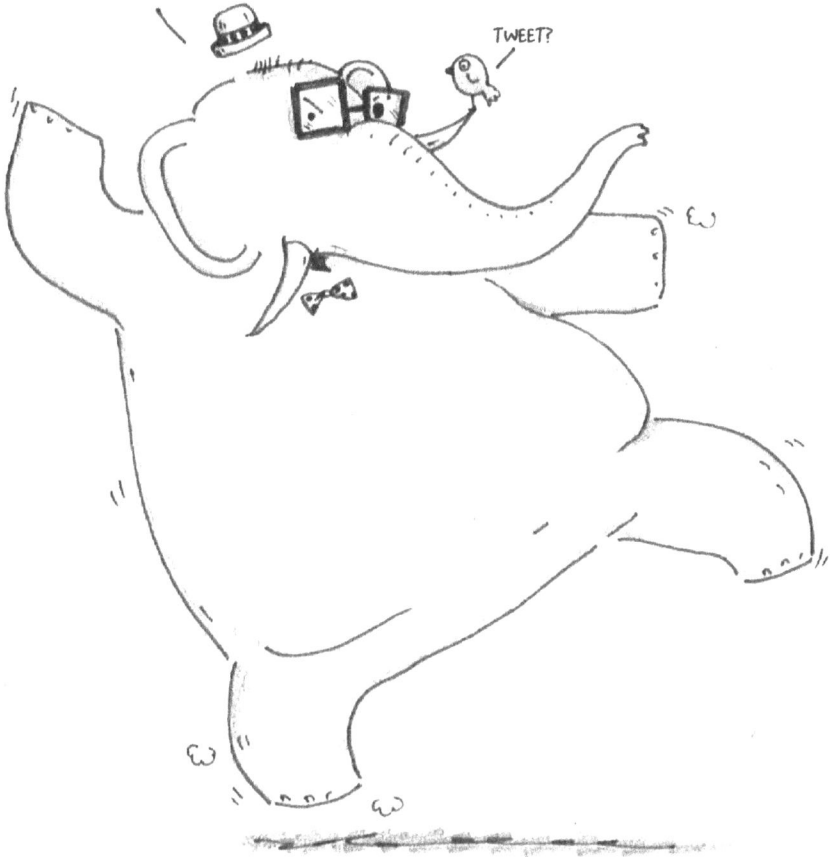

Warriors vs Explorers

Christopher Columbus must have been terrified.

Oh, I am sure he projected an image of being confident about finding a new sea route to India. He obviously projected enough conviction to get sufficient venture capital, sponsors and volunteers for his trip.

But on the inside he must have been terrified. Here he was going against the conventional wisdom that the earth was flat; that if you sailed west from Europe, you would eventually fall off the edge of the earth. His plan was to sail so far west that he would reach the East. How bizarre was that idea? And how much courage does it take to risk all your money, your life and the lives of all your colleagues on an idea?

Especially since his idea was wrong!

Not the idea about the earth being round. That idea had gained some traction in Columbus' time. The idea of the spherical earth had been inferred by the ancient Greeks. In the 2nd century B.C., Eratosthenes, a mathematician who was also a poet, an athlete and a musician, had even worked out the circumference of the earth. His answer was surprisingly close to the correct number, within 1% of the correct answer of 40,000 km.

Columbus' conviction that he could find a sea route to India by sailing west, depended on three assumptions – two of which were wrong. The first was that Columbus thought the earth was much smaller. He thought the earth's circumference was 25,255 km, an error of about 40%. His second error was his belief that there was no land mass between Europe and Asia. His third and only correct belief was that the winds blew over the Atlantic Ocean in a circular pattern and therefore he would be able to take advantage of the winds on his outward as well as return journey.

Columbus was an explorer and an entrepreneur who got lucky. One who made a huge impact on the world – he found a continent that today contributes more than one third of the world's GDP.

That's the kind of impact that explorers make. Way more than warriors. So do you want to be an explorer or a warrior?

Actually, don't answer that question. Let's first examine what makes a warrior successful.

The world's most famous general was Sun Tzu. He was a Chinese general who lived approximately five hundred years before Christ was born. He wrote a book, *The Art of War*, which is still an authoritative book on military strategy. Napoleon, Mao Tse Tung and Ho Chi Minh are few of the great fans of this book. The American Army has prescribed this book as a must read for all its officers and directed that a copy be placed in every library of every unit.

Sun Tzu suggested that the best way to win a war is without fighting it. He said: "To fight and conquer in all your battles is not supreme excellence; supreme excellence consists in breaking the enemy's resistance without fighting."

Sun Tzu is also very clear about if and when an army should fight.

"The art of using troops is this: When ten to the enemy's one, surround him; When five times his strength, attack him; if double his strength, divide him; if equally matched, you may engage him; if weaker numerically, be capable of withdrawing; and, if in all respects unequal, be capable of eluding him, for a small force is but booty for one more powerful."

Yet, marketing has become a testosterone war. How many times have you heard of marketers going head to head with almost identical marketing mixes? Or worse, with lesser resources, but somehow hoping that their bravery (or creativity) would carry them to victory.

Remember the famous poem *Charge of the light brigade*? Lord Tennyson wrote the poignant story of the British cavalry that was outnumbered by the Russians and tried to fight cannons, armed only with swords. One passage:

"Their's not to make reply,
Their's not to reason why,
Their's but to do and die:
Into the valley of Death
Rode the six hundred.

Cannon to right of them,
Cannon to left of them,
Cannon in front of them

Volley'd and thunder'd;
Storm'd at with shot and shell,
Boldly they rode and well,
Into the jaws of Death,
Into the mouth of Hell
Rode the six hundred."

Bravery is all very well. But, except in Bollywood movies, the better-armed army will always beat the brave but foolish one.

In a blog on Huffington Post, Jim Carroll, the UK Chairman of the advertising agency Bartle Bogle Hegarty, wonders why the language of business and war are so similar. He points out:

"Business is all about competition, campaigns and conflicts. We plan offensives, assaults and attacks. We're going into battle, girding our loins, putting boots on the ground. We're employing guerrilla tactics. We're identifying targets and taking aim. We're looking for quick wins, easy wins, win-wins. We're setting up war rooms, playing war games, going on the warpath. We've got to defend our turf. Let's blitz this. We've completed the reconnaissance. We've got the strategic howitzers out. We're addressing the troops. We're giving them their marching orders. We're launching the campaign with shock and awe. It's a full frontal assault, a heavy tonnage media bombardment..."

If we don't use the language of war, then what should we use? The lyricist Jonathan Larson has an interesting point when he says, "The opposite of war isn't peace, it's creation."

In their book, *Blue Ocean Strategy*, W. Chan Kim and Renee Mauborgne have come up with an interesting new metaphor to think about the explorer vs. warrior issue. Large animals fight in the red ocean - the ocean becomes red because of their blood. But there is a large blue ocean out there that is waiting to be conquered by the brave and the innovative.

Red ocean strategies are ones where a warrior goes to conquer a land that is ruled by some other warrior. The only way he can win the war is by fighting it. This is a war that somebody has to lose and somebody has to win. Typically, the war is won by the side with greater resources in terms of men and weapons.

Blue ocean strategies are about discovering and thus conquering new lands. There is usually nobody who is already ruling that space and hence competition is irrelevant. Size of the army is not relevant here - the winner needs to have creativity and courage.

I guess everyone is attracted towards the blue ocean, intuitively. It is the creative route, after all. The problem is that few of us have the courage to be explorers. It is far easier and safer to drive on well paved roads than to trek through unexplored jungles. Even though one knows that the well paved roads are going to be clogged with traffic.

Once you are sick of the traffic and are mentally ready to go onto a new path, you will need a set of tools to use along the way. A sort of a backpack with everything that a budding explorer may need. Not a route map, as it doesn't exist yet, but navigational aids to help find the way. Kim and Mauborgne have attempted to create a bag of these tools in their book.

Let's turn now to our second Guru-speak.

Guru-speak: How to be a Business Explorer

Gautam Buddha, the founder of Buddhism, tried to boil down the essence of his teachings into simple truths and paths. He talked about the 'four noble truths' that he had discovered. In order to rid human beings of suffering, he advocated that we follow the 'eight fold path'.

In their book, *Blue Ocean Strategy*, W. Chan Kim and Renee Mauborgne sound quite like the Buddha as they create their explorer's toolkit. They have six principles and four actions, and six paths in the first principle. Makes innovation seem quite simple. It isn't really, but the tools are interesting and worth learning.

Kim and Mauborgne make a distinction between value creation, innovation and value innovation. Value creation is about lowering costs alone. Innovation focuses on technology without much regard to the costs. Value innovation combines the two, creating a blue ocean strategy.

There are five key differences between a red ocean strategy and a blue ocean one.

Here is the summary of the key differences:

Red Ocean	Blue Ocean
Existing market place	Uncontested market
Beat the competition	Make the competition irrelevant
Exploit existing demand	Create new demand
Make the value-cost trade off	Break the value-cost trade off
Firm strategy: low cost OR differentiation	Firm strategy: low cost AND differentiation

Red ocean strategies are focused on reducing risk, while blue ocean ones are about creating opportunity.

How do you recreate market boundaries? Turns out that there is a checklist that you can work your way through. The authors summarise it in the six paths listed below.

Look Across Alternate Industries

This is the idea of Marketing Myopia that was first proposed by Professor Ted Levitt of Harvard Business School. Prof. Levitt campaigned for a broader definition of business for a firm - not railroads, but transportation; not movies but a night out; not a coffee shop but a third place.

Once you have a broader view, you will see more than just the red ocean around you. That is the insight that led to the success of Starbucks and other coffee shops. They figured that people had a lot of stress, both at work and at home. So they needed a third place where they could hang out and relax. A coffee shop with great coffee, great music, free wifi and a relaxed ambience just about fit the bill.

Was IPL just a cricket tournament? I believe the success of the tournament was at least partly due to its ability to attract some of the movie crazy audience. Here was an entertainment option for the whole family that combined sports, movies, food and music. Once the crowds filled the stadiums, it was easier to make it a hit on TV. Forgotten were the issues about Indian audiences not being interested in domestic cricket, or declining attendance in stadiums when it was so much easier to watch the match in one's living room or the neighbourhood cafe.

Discount airlines don't just get business from other airlines but from customers who use other means of transport. In the USA, these are the people who would have otherwise driven by car. In India, the source of business for discount airlines is train travellers.

Look Across Strategic Groups

If you can't find customers from different industries, perhaps you can find them in different strategic groups. The authors define a strategic group as a set of companies that follow a similar strategy in terms of the price-value trade off. Each of these groups differs so widely from the other that they may as well be in different industries. Mercedes, BMW and Audi form one strategic group, while Honda, Toyota and Ford form a totally different one. Yet, it may be possible for a player in one group to gain business from the other. This was the thought behind the Lexus brand, which offered premium features at a much lower cost.

Discount airlines and full service airlines form distinct strategic groups. The former focusses on people who pay their own fare - small businessmen and people on personal trips. The full service airlines get most of their profits from frequent flyers who travel on company account.

This need to look across strategic groups is particularly important in India and other developing economies. Often the Anglo-Saxon mindset of global companies limits the market for their products.

A good example is of a company that sold home testing kits for diabetes and pregnancy test kits. Typically, one set of companies caters to the home market and another to the pathology labs market. However, in India, the pathology lab is often a small shop in a residential area run by a paramedic as a stand-alone business. Patients in India value the convenience and the cost advantage of these labs and often prefer them to larger labs as well as home test kits. The global company that sold home kits had to reorient it's thinking to deal with the labs rather than with end customers.

Look Across the Buyer Chain

If you can't find customers in a different industry or a different part of your industry, look across the chain of buyers and influencers. Novo Nordisk did this successfully. Their product is a "pen" that is used to inject insulin in diabetes patients. It is much smaller, easier and more convenient than a syringe. Typically, such products are marketed to doctors who prescribe them to their patients. However, Novo Nordisk reached out directly to patients and got them to ask their doctors to prescribe the pens. Similarly, Bloomberg marketed its terminals to the end users - the traders rather than the IT managers.

In many categories, we see the pester power of kids and teenagers. In a study that we did at Euro RSCG in India, we found that the younger generation not only affected the brand choices for the products that they used, but also affected their parents' choice of products like mutual funds they were considering to invest in.

Another insight we discovered was in the context of an anti-osteoporosis program. The incidence of osteoporosis in post-menopausal women is over 50%. Yet, it's almost impossible to get Indian women to sign on to and stick to a program that will prevent the disease. We found that a better route was to talk to their children. It was easier to convince successful young professionals to prevail upon their mothers than to overcome the sacrificial mindset of the older Indian women.

Look Across Complimentary Products and Services

The definition of what a company sells keeps getting wider and wider. At one time, the product was basically what the factory produced. Later, an emotional layer got attached to it. "In the factory we produce cosmetics, in the store we sell hope," said Charles Revson, the founder of Revlon Cosmetics. Now the retail experience and other ancillary services like financing have become an integral part of any brand.

Financing schemes have become key in many product categories like automobiles and durables. Tata Motors used finance as a tool to beat back the strong competition from Japanese brands in the light trucks segment in the 1990s. They offered more flexibility in installment amounts as well as more convenience in terms of collection points.

The success of the iPod is due to the seamless integration of the hardware, software and the music store. Similarly, the Amazon Kindle integrates hardware, software and a book purchase store. This has now become the norm and other hardware manufacturers are trying to create integrated solutions for customers too. This is a far cry from the Wintel era where everyone expected that manufacturers would specialise in just one layer of the product, leaving the onus of integrating the package on the customer.

The focus is increasingly on the complete consumer experience. The Paris metro system, RATP, redesigned the entire chain of touch points with its travelers. This involved creating a better ambience at the stations with art exhibitions and music, bicycles that you could hire for going short distances from the station and a newspaper to read on the trains. Of course, the ticket buying process and the actual train travel were improved too.

Look Across Functional or Emotional Appeals

There seems to be a cycle where categories move from rational product appeals to emotional ones and then back again. Swatch turned a functional industry into a fashion one. Body Shop did the reverse. Each of them created a blue ocean strategy.

Swatch went anti-clockwise of Swiss watch manufacturers. The others made heirloom watches that lasted for generations. These were expensive, handcrafted, made of gold or other precious metals and consumers were expected to own just one. Swatch made cheap plastic watches that were colourful and fashionable. They were cheap, consumers could own several and match them with their outfits. In fact, the first big marketing initiative that Swatch did was to create a huge watch that hung down the side of the tallest building in Zurich, which proudly proclaimed, 'Swatch. Swiss made. SFr 15.'

The Body Shop operated in a category that sold dreams and imagery. Brands spent more money on packaging and advertising than on making the actual product. The Body Shop decided to have plain packaging for its products and no advertising. The brand stood for functional benefits from its products and combined that with higher order values such as a strong stance against animal testing and later against the myths of globalisation.

We will see later in the book that this social aspect of brands is a new and useful dimension to compete on. Maybe, in the future, there will be other dimensions on which brands will compete. But it is interesting to note how the dominant theme in a category can switch quickly from functional to emotional and back.

Look Across Time

Most successful explorers are somewhat clairvoyant. They can see into the future and anticipate it. This is the basis for blue ocean strategists too.

Steve Jobs was surely a genius in that respect. His ability to predict the future has led to the success of Apple in products like the iPod, the iPhone and the iPad. In the case of the iPod, he saw that there would be a market for legal music downloads even though most of the music was illegally downloaded at that time. He predicted that the future of magazines and books lay in devices such as the iPad. Reading addicts like me are rapidly filling up their iPads with books, magazines, RSS feeds and the like.

Amitabh Bachchan says he did not create the persona of the angry young man. His team and he merely saw the emerging trend in Indian society and depicted this trend in memorable movies that turned him into the biggest superstar that the Indian movie industry has ever seen. Of course, the movies fed fuel to the trend and set up a vicious cycle that helped the success of this genre of movies.

These paths would certainly help achieve brand nirvana.

Let me turn now to sports - an arena where the war metaphor is constantly used. Even here, a valuable brand has succeeded by doing something different.

Sports and the War Metaphor

Emotions are high when India plays Pakistan in cricket. As they are when England plays Australia or even when Yorkshire plays Lancashire (that last is called the War of Roses). In football, there are several encounters that always get the police on edge. Matches like Real Madrid vs. FC Barcelona, Manchester United vs. Manchester City or ever our own East Bengal vs. Mohun Bagan. Some football matches have even resulted in riots among the fans.

In sports, there is a winner and a loser. As there is in war. It is not surprising then that the war metaphor is so often used in the context of sports. Often, the sporting conflict is a reflection of rivalries in the real world. It is not surprising that a lot of the sporting wars are fought between neighbours.

Clearly, the war metaphor works for sports. It has been used to promote all kinds of sports in all countries across the world. Is it even possible to create a sporting event that is not based on a war?

I will argue in this piece that the Indian Premier League (IPL) does not owe its popularity to war but to voyeurism.

Domestic cricket started in India in the pre independence era when different communities played each other in local tournaments. Thus, the Bombay tournament was called the Pentangular and was played between the Hindus, the Muslims, the Europeans, the Parsis and the rest. This tournament ran from the year 1912 to the year 1936. It was opposed by Mahatma Gandhi on the grounds that it divided the country and created too much passion that was misplaced. It was replaced by the Ranji Trophy that is played between state teams and continues till today.

However, the Ranji Trophy has never been able to create the kind of passion that the Pentangular did. The historian Ramachandra Guha has written about the contrast between the two tournaments in his book, *A Corner of a Foreign Field*. He vividly contrasts the crowds at the Brabourne stadium for the final match of the Pentangular between Hindus and Muslims against a major Ranji Trophy match at the same ground where Bombay was one of the teams. When you read the comparison, you can't help but feel that sporting contests need the spice of real world conflict to be popular.

When the Indian Premier League was first mooted as a contest between eight domestic clubs, most people expected it to be a flop. If people were not interested in a Ranji Trophy match between Mumbai and Delhi, why should there be any interest in a match between Mumbai Indians and Delhi Daredevils? Especially if players from Delhi could be playing for the Mumbai club and vice versa. It was most confusing.

The IPL turned out to be a huge financial success. But where did the experts go wrong? The experts failed because they evaluated IPL as a domestic cricket tournament. The IPL was not just a cricket tournament. It was charting the blue ocean territory by creating a whole new genre of entertainment.

IPL is a cross between a cricket tournament and a TV reality show. Everything about it is about entertainment. The televised auction of the players; the huge monies; the involvement of big business houses, their leaders and big movie stars; the cheerleaders and the music on the grounds; the timing and the length of the matches (prime time and for three hours each - the same length as a Hindi movie); the after match parties; and, of course, the scandals.

In fact, a bit more about the scandals -those add real spice to the whole show! In the first IPL tournament, Harbhajan Singh slapped Sreesanth. It led to a string of scandals and controversies that have included court cases, arrests, allegations about drug usage, star fights and so on. This isn't cricket as played on the grounds of Eton or watched at Lords. This is more like a masala Hindi movie, which has a bit of every kind of emotion. The IPL dominated every section of the newspaper from the front page to the business page to the social pages; and, of course, the sports pages.

The IPL is the first sporting event in the world where the primary metaphor is not that of war. The rivalries between the teams have been subsumed by the rivalries between the movie stars, the businessmen and individual players. In marketing and business terms, this was pure genius. No wonder that Lalit Modi, the first commissioner of the IPL, was honored as the 'Marketer of the Year' by a trade publication of the advertising and marketing industry.

The cricket puritan in me is appalled at how this noble game has changed. The marketer in me is totally in awe. From zero to a brand valuation of USD four billion in just three years is an amazing achievement.

Since the removal of Lalit Modi from the boss-man's seat, the IPL has tried to focus a bit more on cricket. This led to a decline in TV ratings. The people who run this tournament have to realize that IPL isn't just about cricket.

My Enemy is my Friend

"Adam Smith needs revision," said John Nash in the movie Beautiful Mind. He probably said it in real life too. Prof. Nash then proceeded to revise one of the key principles of Adam Smith's theories. And in doing so, laid down the foundations of a field of economics called the game theory. This field is so important that so far eight Nobel Prizes in Economics have been given for work in this area.

Like with all powerful theories, the basic idea is simple and elegant. Adam Smith said that every man must think for himself and try to maximize his own gains. Game theory says that sometimes working for the common good is better than working for personal gain. Thus, it ends up teaching us that sometimes cooperating with our competitors leads to greater benefits for everyone. Thus, it changes the whole idea that marketing is all about war.

Let's go back to the scene from the movie that I quoted at the beginning of this article (you could watch it by going to http://youtube/uAJDD1_Oexo). The scene is set in a bar where John Nash and his friends are drinking. A group of girls enter the bar and one girl, 'the blonde', is clearly better looking than the rest. This is where Nash explains his idea of game theory.

The first reaction of all the boys is to go for the blonde. John Nash explains that by competing against each other, they will cancel each other out. They can all then go for the other girls, but will probably get rebuffed since no one likes being a second choice.

However, what if everyone decides to not go for the blonde but go directly for the other girls. In that case, they can all get dates and be better off rather than pursuing their selfish interest.

This principle, where competitors cooperate with each other for mutual benefit, has spawned a lot of ugly sounding words like coopetition, frenemy and the like. Ugly words or not, the idea has created profits for competitors in various fields.

Thus, car makers have started to share parts and even entire car bodies. PSA Citroen and Toyota share car parts that go into their respective city cars - the Peugeot 107, the Toyota Aygo and the Citroën C1. Similarly, between the

Suman Srivastava

years 1991 and 1998, Volkswagen and Ford produced one car body in their joint venture plant in Portugal and sold it as Sharan (Volkswagen), Galaxy (Ford) and Alhambra (Seat/Volkswagen).

Cell phone service operators share cell phone towers, while internet service providers share underground cables. Towers and cables had started out as the basis of competition among these players. Cell phone companies used to compete on better coverage on the basis that one had more towers than the other. This basis of competition led to all players losing money. It made more sense to share the infrastructure and find other ways to compete in the consumer's mind.

Mobile phone operators in India have been smarter. They cooperated with each other to get government policies changed in ways that benefitted all of them. In the early days, a flat license fee was payable for each circle by the operators to the government. This led to huge losses for the operators. They got together as the Cellular Operators Association of India and lobbied with the government to move from a flat fee regime to one based on revenue percentage. This policy helped them to survive and subsequently created a boom in the mobile phone market in India. In effect, it made the cake larger and sweeter for everybody.

Even apparently competitive situations offer a lot of scope for cooperation. In their book on game theory called *The Art of Strategy*, Professors Avinash Dixit and Barry Nalebuff have a case study on the bidding for spectrum among cell phone operators. Of course, collusion between competitors is prohibited in such auctions. But they are able to show mathematically that competitors can end up collaborating for better profits for both.

The key here is that bidding for spectrum is actually several games rolled into one. At the simplest level, think of two players bidding for two cities. Imagine if one of them is clearly the stronger player and can bid more in both the cities and consequently, wins both the cities. Yet, the professors prove that the stronger company would make better profit if it wins only one city at a lower price and allows the other player to win the other city.

Game theory is a bit like quantum mechanics in Physics. Like the latter, game theory is counter intuitive. Like quantum mechanics, it gives us greater insights. Both these theories are equally fascinating.

Time for another Guru-speak.

Guru-Speak: Strategic Games

Professor Avinash Dixit is supposed to be a playful man. A fitting trait for a person who is one of the global experts in the field of game theory. He teaches at the Princeton University, where it is tradition for students to applaud when a teacher finishes a course for them. Prof. Dixit offers to pay a small sum of money to the student who ends up clapping till the last. This little game has ensured that he always gets a long round of applause, with the record being four and a half hours (as reported by the Mint newspaper). Sounds like fun; I must try it sometime.

In their book, *The Art of Strategy*, Avinash Dixit and Barry Nalebuff write a wonderful definition of strategy:

> "We started the original preface with: Strategic thinking is the art of outdoing an adversary, knowing that the adversary is trying to do the same to you. To this we now add: It is also the art of finding ways to cooperate, even when others are motivated by self-interest not benevolence. It is the art of convincing others, and even yourself, to do what you say. It is the art of interpreting and revealing information. It is the art of putting yourself in others' shoes so as to predict and influence what they will do."

Given this, how does one go about creating marketing strategies? Or any other strategies, for that matter. Professors Dixit and Nalebuff have some nice lessons, some of them counter intuitive, to share with us in their book. In the first chapter, they talk about ten stories that illustrate their lessons. I shall briefly talk about those ten principles.

Put Yourself in the Other Player's Shoes

Steve Ballmer of Microsoft likes to play a game in interviews to check if a candidate has a logical way of thinking. He thinks of a number between one and hundred and asks the candidate to guess it in the fewest possible guesses. Each time that they guess, he will tell them if they are too low or too high. Now the best way to do this is to choose the middle number of the available range each time. So your first guess should be fifty, if that's too high, then twenty five, if that's too low, thirty seven, still too low, then forty three and so on.

This is great, but if you know the other guy is going to do this, then the best number for you to guess may well be forty nine so that it takes a really long time for the other person to guess.

Think Like a Chess Player

The difference between an ordinary chess player and a good one is the ability to foresee the best moves that both sides can make. The better the player, the further he can think. In game theory, it is necessary to be able to think several steps ahead to the final outcome. The authors talk about the final rounds of a reality TV show, Survivor, where three players, Richard, Rudy and Kelly, were in the penultimate round. The rules of the game were such that the player who won that round could choose one of the losers to compete against in the final. They show us the way Richard thought through his options. Rudy was the most popular with the audience, so neither of the other players could have won against him in the final. However, if Richard won the semi final and did not choose Rudy, the latter's supporters would have been disappointed and would have voted against Richard. So the best option for Richard was to hope Kelly won the round and selected to play against him in the final. Which is what happened, leading to his winning the prize.

Your Weakness can Help you Win

In professional sports, players keenly analyse the strengths and weaknesses of their opponents. If you have a strong forehand in tennis, opponents will play to your backhand. So, you will need to improve your backhand in order to win. If you improve your backhand enough, then the play would be equal on both sides and you will actually be able to use your stronger side more and win.

In team sports like football, blocking the strongest player in the opposing team often leads to openings for other players to sneak through and score. Thus, it is best not to assume that the only way to win is with your trump card.

Follow the Follower

Games aren't always about winning in every round. Sometimes, it is necessary to lose the battle to win the war. In marketing, we know of the first mover disadvantage where the pioneer ends up making mistakes early or just paves the way for later players to come in and take over the market. Unilever certainly believes in the second mover or fast follower advantage.

Be Selectively Flexible

Negotiations seem to be all about taking a tough stand. Certainly there are many stories about people who got what they wanted by taking up a position and sticking to it. This may work in the short run, but probably won't in the long run. Your opponents will think you are greedy and not want to negotiate with you in the future; or they would come up with their own tough stances to try and make up for ground lost in the previous round. So it is crucial to be selectively flexible.

Reduce your Options

If you are dieting, you have to fight yourself. It is the pleasure of having dessert now versus the pleasure of looking good sometime in the future. The present self wins out often. In cases like this, you may need to play games that help you be strong today.

The authors helped design a show called *Life: The Game*, where participants who wanted to lose weight put themselves in a bind that they could get out of only by dieting. One participant posed in a bikini while she was overweight and signed off a release that said her pictures could be aired if she did not lose a certain amount of weight before a cut off date. She made it even worse for herself by getting a friend to promise to ask an ex-boyfriend to see the show where those pictures would be shown. The only way to not be embarrassed would be to lose weight and that's what she did.

Generals are known to burn the bridges by which they have come or ships on which they have travelled to ensure that their men understand that there is no option other than winning. If they lose, they have nowhere to run. It increases their chances of victory.

Play the Right Game

You not only need to play the game well, you need to play the right game. Some situations are such that the best result for each player leads to a sub optimal result for the group as a whole. This is what we referred to in the previous chapter.

In the book, there is a delightful idea of how to get political parties in a democracy to do something that is good for society, but not good for the politicians. The authors talk about campaign funding reform. It is good for society if the whole method of funding elections is changed so that big money does not influence the elections. However, such a bill will never pass through the parliament of any democratic country, as the politicians got there because of their ability to raise big money. If they pass such a law, then they will stand to lose.

The authors suggest that Warren Buffett (or some other billionaire) should offer a large amount of money to the party that provides the most votes for the bill. Now both parties would be in a dilemma. They don't want to pass the bill, but they don't want the other party to support it either. Their ideal solution would be to vote for the bill and have the opposing party defeat it. Thus, they would make money but also not have the law. However, since both parties have the same strategy, they will end up passing the bill. Wonderful!

The Importance of Being Random

Game theory is all about playing percentages. If you are going to shoot a penalty kick in football and you know that the goalkeeper is weak on his left side, should you always kick to that side? If you do, the goalkeeper will be able to second guess you and save the kick. So your best strategy may be that 70% of the time you kick to the goalkeeper's left and 30% to his right. This way he will stay honest. That does not mean that you should kick to the left the first seven times and to the right the next three times. You have to find a way to randomise your strategy so that the goalkeeper is kept guessing.

Similarly, in cricket, an off spinner may get a lot of wickets with his 'doosra' (the ball that spins the other way). The question is when and how often he should bowl it? If the bowler becomes too predictable, the batsmen will not get out.

The great Indian leg spinner Chandrashekhar used to say that he himself didn't know what kind of a delivery he would be bowling until his arm had gone up to actually bowl the ball. So there was no way for the batsman to guess what ball was coming at him. Perhaps, that is why Chandrashekhar was so successful.

The Importance of Losing Occasionally

If you are gambling and only bid when you have great cards, then other players will soon figure it out and not bid when you start bidding. To make money on the table, it is important to bid sometimes when you have bad cards. Not only that, you must also be seen as bidding with bad cards so that your opponents can't figure out whether you are bluffing or not.

There is Always a Larger Game

In some of the lessons above, the authors have alluded to the fact that the current game might be just one round in a longer game. This point is different; it says that there may be an altogether different game being played that you need to be aware of. In an example in the book, Barry talks about a fight between him and a taxi driver in Israel. Turns out that actually the cabbie wasn't just fighting with Barry, he was trying to not lose face in front of his girlfriend.

Companies and brands sometimes behave 'irrationally' due to the egos of their CEOs. I read an article recently that said that CEOs who appear on magazine covers are more likely to pay exorbitant prices to buy another company.

Game theory is a fascinating subject. Moreover, it is a technical subject. Several Nobel Prizes in Economics have been won by people who have made contributions to this subject. Finally, game theory does not just have to do with economics, but with all aspects of life including marketing.

ELEPHANT IN THE ROOM:

CONSUMERS ARE NOT RATIONAL

That Crazy Number THREE!

Next time you are in a large group (more than thirty people), try this experiment. Write down number three on a piece of paper, fold it and give it to any one person to keep without looking at it. Ask everyone to write down any one of the numbers from one to four. Collect the slips and count the number of people who chose each of the numbers. You will find that most of the people will choose the number three. Now ask the person holding on to your piece of paper to reveal its content. Magic!

Weird, isn't it? But wait, it gets more interesting. Have you noticed that in religion, the number three keeps popping up? First of all, there are three major streams of religions - the Abrahamic religions, the Dharmic religions and the Taoic religions.

And within individual religions, you see the number three taking center stage. Christianity has the Holy Trinity of the father, son and the holy-spirit. The Holy family had three members, Joseph, Mary and Jesus. When Jesus was born, three wise men appeared and left him three gifts.

Hinduism has the Trimurti consisting of Brahma, Vishnu and Shiva; and Shiva carries the trishul. In Islam, the hands, arms, feet and face have to be washed three times before each prayer. Buddhists take refuge in the three jewels - Buddha, Dharma and Sangha.

Let's move on to other fields. In fairy tales, genies always grant you three wishes. And quite often, the Kings in these stories have three sons or three daughters. There are three primary colours that combine to form all the other ones. While in Baseball, three strikes and a batter is out, and when three batters are out, the innings is over. In cricket, we celebrate a hat-trick, but don't even have a name for four or more wickets in a row.

So what is happening here? Why did people choose three instead of any of the other numbers? Notice that the choice was only among four numbers, so there is no bias towards the center. Notice also that most people would like to be first in whatever they do, and yet they end up choosing number three even though they had the option of choosing number one.

Apart from three, there is another mystical number. That is the number seven. There are seven days in a week and there are seven notes in music. There are seven wonders of the world and Snow White met seven dwarfs. There are many references to the number seven in the Harry Porter series of books (there are seven books in all, by the way) and it is considered a magical number. They say that you can only remember up to seven things in a list. If there are more, you need to break them up into two or more lists.

There is no logical reason for the dominance of these two numerals over all the others. It just so happens. Most of the time we don't even stop to think about it. And if someone points out this peculiarity to us, we just smile, shrug and move on. We just can't understand it.

Which is the point I wish to make. There is a lot about us that we cannot understand. We don't really understand how and why we take decisions, including marketing decisions. We know that only a small part of our brain is occupied with rational or conscious thought. The rest is irrational or unconscious.

And yet we assume that consumers are rational; that they take decisions in a rational manner and maximise their utility function.

How crazy are we?

Philosophers and wits from down the ages have been disputing the notion that human beings are rational beings. Aristotle and Descartes both considered the idea that human beings were 'rational animals', but discarded the thought. Later, Bertrand Russell said, "It has been said that man is a rational animal. All my life I have been searching for evidence which could support this."

Oscar Wilde said it in a wittier fashion: "Man is a rational animal who always loses his temper when called upon to act in accordance with the dictates of reason."

In spite of the best advice of philosophers down the ages, economists insist on assuming that human beings are rational at least in their economic decisions.

The Seductive Utility Function

Don't you just love Asterix? And Obelix, even more? He is constantly surprised by how crazy the Romans are. In one instance, he went a step further and concluded, "These humans are crazy."

Well, of course we are. All humans are crazy, at least in real life. Efforts are made in movies and in commercials to depict heroes as perfect, but we never like those characters anyway. The people we like have lovable imperfections.

The greatest books, the greatest plays and the greatest movies are all about people with that little quirk that helps create the story. Shakespeare was a master in creating heroes with a tragic flaw.

We know that people fall in love, fall out of love, fight, get excited, get depressed, become fans and become enemies for the most irrational reasons.

Which is why it comes as such a surprise that Economics has lived with the assumption of rationality for so long. Long ago, Economics made the assumption that all humans are rational actors whose main aim in life is to maximise their utility function. This means that they rationally evaluate all the options available to them and make their choices in such a way as to further their selfish interests.

When you say it like that, it sounds so wrong! We know that people are capable of doing quite unselfish things. We give to charity. We give up our seats for others. We allow that little hawker at the signal to cheat us just so he gains the self esteem of earning his living. Soldiers sacrifice their lives just to save the life of a comrade.

Even in our economic lives, we don't behave rationally. We don't always buy the cheapest product that we could. Sometimes, we buy luxury goods that are clearly over-priced for irrational reasons like status or some other feel-good factor. Often, we buy things we don't need, just because there is a 'Sale' sticker on them.

Given all this, why have economists and marketers stuck with the assumption of rationality? The short answer is that the economists needed the assumption to create models of consumer behaviour. The mathematics of irrationality would make your head ache. It is far easier to draw 'revealed utility' curves for each consumer, assume that they all seek to maximise these functions and, therefore, conclude that society is happiest when the maximum number of people are at the outer boundaries of their utility functions. Economists did just that and it worked fine for them.

Marketers simply followed the economists. We could all sit in our offices and assume that if our product was little better than that of our competitors, then consumers would buy our product. We assumed that making the price a little lower, or the product a little tastier or the packaging a little more colourful would make all the difference. And we were caught by surprise when consumers didn't flock to our brands. It is no wonder that most marketers sneer at the foolishness of the consumers.

But now, economists are coming to the rescue of marketers. A whole new branch is evolving that is called Behavioural Economics. This new science starts by dropping the two assumptions that I have been railing against in this piece. They no longer assume that consumers are rational or that they seek to maximise their utility function.

So what happens when you drop these two assumptions? Fun things, really. Suddenly, the picture clears up and the snow vanishes from the screen. The hiss vanishes from the audio. We can see and hear clearly; and what we see and hear is often surprising.

Guru-Speak: This New Economics is Not Dismal

To be fair, economists have never really believed that consumers are rational. They just needed to make that assumption to create mathematical economic models. But a new breed of economists is challenging this thinking. They are creating a new branch of their science that is called Behavioural Economics. This new science drops two major assumptions that the standard economic models make. These assumptions are: unbounded rationality and unbounded selfishness.

When you see the assumptions listed like that you are entitled to wonder what kind of imbeciles made them in the first place! How could anyone ever believe that human beings behave all the time in a perfectly rational and selfish way? Sometimes, we are both, sometimes one or the other, and sometimes none. The challenge is for the economists and the marketers to figure out how to adapt their models to take into account this capricious behaviour.

Behavioural economists are coming up with some interesting insights based on observations and devised experiments. One of the gurus of this new field is Dan Ariely. His book, *Predictably Irrational*, introduced me to this field and made me realise the necessity of changing our marketing tactics to bring them in line with the new science. These insights ring true and often bring forth a smile of recognition. Though much more work remains to be done, it is useful to look at a few of these tenets.

Change the Frame of Reference

Money is an arbitrary scale. Human beings actually cannot assign monetary values to a product or service. The only way to do so is with reference to something else. However, once the reference is established, it is set forever.

It is similar to an animal, a tiger cub brought up by a dog for example. The cub will accept the dog as its mother. This is true for all creatures. I read recently of a baby hippo that was brought up by a tortoise. This is called the Gosling Effect or Arbitrary Coherence. The opportunity for marketers is to create new frames of reference for their products.

A brilliant example of great marketing comes from Mark Twain's classic, *Tom Sawyer*. In the story, Tom had to paint a fence, which he obviously didn't want to do. So he managed to convince his friends that painting was a super fun activity. In the end, he had a line of kids paying him for a chance to paint a section of the fence. Not only did Tom not have to do the work, he even earned some money while not doing it. All by changing the reference from a chore to a fun activity.

Another way of changing the frame of reference is to do a sale. Having a price tag that says an original price as well as a sale price is so much more powerful than just giving the final lower price. This is the insight that shoe shops on Linking Road in Bandra use. These shops seem to be on perpetual sale. Even the banners announcing the sale are old and faded. Yet, consumers take comfort in buying shoes at a price that is supposedly lower than the full price.

Creating a new frame of reference often requires creating a relationship with an existing category. When cars were invented, consumers didn't know what they were. So they were referred to as horseless carriages. We see many categories with adjectives describing the product - flat televisions, sonic toothbrushes, cordless phones.

The new category forces the consumers to drop their mental anchors for prices. They are now open to the Gosling effect and will accept a new price point. Once established, all other players have to stick close to the new anchor.

Make Relativity Work to your Advantage

A special case of changing the reference is to use decoy options in pricing. Ariely gives the example of The Economist. They offered two options to subscribers. One was a web subscription for USD 57 and a print subscription for USD 125. When faced with such an option, most net savvy people would choose the web option.

Now, introduce a third option - both the web and print editions for USD 125. This makes the print only option a dummy offer. You would expect that introducing the third option would not matter to those who want the web subscription, and only the people who prefer print would now gravitate to the new offer.

However, that was not the case; an overwhelming majority of people chose the web plus print option. Why would that be?

Dan Ariely and his team have been able to replicate the above example numerous times. In each case, they first offer two choices that are pretty similar to each other – calling them A and B. The respondents are always evenly split between those two options. Then they introduce the dummy option, which is clearly inferior to one of the offers (say B), calling it C. Each time they found that respondents started choosing option B more. In fact, so long as C was similar but inferior to B, the latter would get chosen. So much for the rational man!

Ariely uses the insight above to recommend that young people seeking a date would do well to hang out with someone who is similar but slightly inferior to them. It improves the chances of getting a date.

We love keeping options open. We hate to commit ourselves and sometimes pay a price for it. Marketers need to help the consumer take a decision. The dummy option is one way to help consumers decide.

Sell for Free

Of course, everyone loves getting something for free. Duh! What's so special about that?

Well, this is where irrationality really comes into its own. Human beings will give up good value just to take something that is free. Dan Ariely's classic experiment involved a special chocolate treat and an ordinary chocolate. At first, people were asked to pay for both -thirty cents for the special treat and one cent for the ordinary one. At this point, most people chose the special treat, since it was better value. Then, the price of both was reduced by a penny each, making the ordinary one free. Rationally, this should not have made any difference to people's choices. If anything, the better chocolate was now even more of a deal. But this time, most people took the free option.

Why is this? Perhaps, it is because human beings hate losing more than they like winning. So, when they get an option where they cannot lose, they take it. Even if it means they lose a potential winner. As observers, we can only shake our heads in amusement.

People will do almost anything to get something for free, including spending a lot of money. Thus, consumers will buy that extra book from Amazon just to qualify for free shipping. In stores, they will buy three garments instead of one, just so that they qualify for the fourth free one.

Chris Anderson has written a book called *Free* that describes how the modern world is moving towards a free economy. He outlines numerous business models that offer something for free while making money for the promoters of the company. To begin with, Mr. Anderson offers his book for free if you want to download it as a PDF. However, if you want a physical copy or even a Kindle version, then you need to pay for it. And, of course, you need to pay if you want him to consult with your company or want him to speak at your conference. That is one kind of a free model. Lets call it the loss leader model - you lose money on one product (the book) while you make money on other related products like the consultancy and the talks. This kind of a middle path is probably the way forward for the music industry. Artists will not earn as much from their CD sales as they used to; perhaps, the norm would be to give the music away for free and make money on the concerts and the merchandizing.

The most common free model is the media model. Media channels get paid by advertisers for producing content that is consumed by the public. You and I don't pay for media - or pay very little for it. Think of newspapers that cost us a fraction of their production cost, radio that comes streaming down for free or Google that provides wonderful services for free.

There are other models too. See the chapter titled, 'Pricing mysteries that will make your head itch' for more examples.

Pricing used to be a simple exercise of adding on a profit margin over the costs. Now, it is as creative a field as advertising.

Use Social Norms

Rational human beings should charge money for everything. They should not do anything for free. So if you go to someone's place for dinner, expect to get a bill at the end of the evening.

I don't know about you, but I actually know one such person. Fortunately, he is the only one among my thousands of acquaintances who would do so. Consequently, we try to keep interactions with him at a minimum as all of us live in a social world, which is different from the world of markets.

I often speak at colleges and management schools. So far, I have never charged money for these talks. However, I do accept small gifts like a book or a tie. Imagine if the school were to offer me INR 500 in cash instead of that gift. Wouldn't I feel insulted? Yet, that is the value of the book and the tie, and I am quite happy with them.. I'm not very rational, am I?

People who work in the armed forces and the fire department aren't very rational either. The money they make is probably not worth the risks they take. But they are all working for a higher cause - to defend the nation or to save people in trouble.

Dan Ariely has rightly said: "Money, it turns out, is very often the most expensive way to motivate people. Social norms are not only cheaper, but often more effective as well."

Combining the social world with the market world sounds like a great idea but it is a difficult tool to handle. The telecom company, Aircel, ran a very visible campaign about saving the tiger. However, nobody could figure out what to do to save the tiger and what the linkage was with Aircel or mobile phones. The brand came through as opportunistic, even manipulative.

It is also crucial to be consistent with social messaging for a long period of time. Flitting from social to market and back is a recipe for disaster. Ariely has a great story about this.

A day care center in Israel found that parents were often late in coming to pick up their children after school. The parents would be apologetic about the delay but that didn't help the school from incurring extra costs for the delay. So, the school decided to impose a monetary fine on parents who came late. They hoped that this would deter parents from coming late. However, the opposite happened. Now that parents were paying for the longer hours, they were free of any guilt. They could come as late as they liked.

The kicker in this story is that when the school decided to scrap the fine, parents did not go back to their original behaviour but continued coming late. The moral of the story is that flitting from social to the market world and back is not desirable.

This may sound obvious, but we violate this principle quite often. Companies, for instance, talk about their employees being family. But then they go ahead and fire people at the first sign of trouble. You don't fire family members, do you? If you want loyalty from your people, then you have to be loyal to them too.

Get People into the Mood First

Emotions trump rationality. There is a whole genre of crime fiction based only on this insight - where people commit murder because they are crazed by passion. It is clear that emotions make us do things we wouldn't otherwise do.

Back to Dan Ariely and team. They did a series of studies in college campuses where they got respondents to answer questions while they masturbated! They compared these responses with answers from the same people when they were not so aroused. The difference was stark.

There are several cases of brands that have used 'non-rational' sensory experiences to influence consumers. We will see examples of these in the next few chapters.

Order People to Behave

We love to procrastinate. Especially on things that we know we should be doing. That's why God made parents. Their job is to tell us what to do and then follow up with us to ensure that we have done it. That's also the job of bosses in the office.

Once we enter adulthood and are on our own, we still need someone to order us around. That seems to improve our behaviour. Dan Ariely decided to test the hypothesis that people perform better when they are under some kind of external control, rather than when they have complete freedom.

Prof. Ariely's course required students to submit three projects during the term. He used this for his experiment. He divided the students into three sections. He offered one section complete freedom by letting them submit their projects anytime before the last day of the term. He offered no flexibility to the second group of students - he gave them fixed dates for submissions and laid down penalties for delay. To the third group, he offered a planning tool. He told them that they had to set their own deadlines for each project and specify those dates by the end of the first week. The deadlines could be any time before the end of the term. There was no problem in submitting the projects early, but delays would attract a penalty.

At the end of the term, he looked at the grades that each group of students got. The best grades were earned by the students with no flexibility. The worst grades were from the students who had complete flexibility. However, the third group with options did somewhere in between. This shows that even little help in planning could help reduce procrastination and improve performance.

It's the same with life. We all intend to do some good deeds but often don't because nobody is following up.

Intel used this insight to push people into buying home PCs in India. Research showed that people who planned to buy computers and could afford them as well, never got around to actually buying. Perhaps, falling prices were a problem? You could always get a better deal if you waited. So how could Intel get consumers to stop procrastinating?

I worked on the Intel brand in India during this time as my agency, Euro RSCG, handled their business then. We decided to impose a deadline on consumers. We found that education was the biggest reason for buying a computer, so we told parents that they should buy a PC before their child reaches class nine. Else, they are putting their child at a disadvantage compared to his or her peers. This strategy worked well for Intel and the campaign won huge internal accolades including an award that is referred to as Intel's 'internal Nobel'. This prize is usually given to technology projects and rarely to marketing ones. Indeed, it was a huge honour for the team to receive this prize.

I used this technique in my personal life too. I have never been much of an athlete. I have always hated running as a sport. Moreover, I was forty five and unfit and couldn't run even hundred meters without panting when I decided to run the half marathon. Not only did I set myself this goal, I announced this to all my friends and family. I even wrote it on my Facebook page and tweeted about it. This pressure that I put myself under ensured that I dragged myself out of bed on days that I didn't feel like training. It also helped me get over the mental barriers that prevent us from achieving what our bodies are capable of.

Create No-Lose Situations

Human beings are an acquisitive species. We love everything that belongs to us and hate to throw away anything. We just have to look at all the junk that we collect in forgotten corners of our home to verify this hypothesis. We are so acquisitive that we assign much higher values to what we own than what it deserves. The funny thing is that this change happens in just an instant. One moment you are looking at this curio and wondering whether it is worth the price. The next moment you buy it and become over possessive about it and scream if someone doesn't handle it properly.

This is why sellers of houses value their house way higher than buyers. Buyers are relatively more objective. They know the market price and can see all the good things and the bad things in the house to reach a fair valuation.

The seller is selling their home, which they transformed from a house. In their mind, this house is way better than the one next door, even though both may look similar and the neighbour's house has a new coat of paint.

If simple ownership doesn't make you possessive, then a little bit of work certainly will. Everyone believes that they make the best cocktails in the world - I certainly do. There isn't much skill involved in making a cocktail. Essentially, you are throwing a few ingredients together and stirring them. Small changes in proportions will make no discernible difference in the taste. Yet, we think that we make the best cocktails.

Ikea uses this insight very well. You have to assemble an Ikea product yourself. And the simple act of bolting on the legs to a table-top makes you feel as if you made the table yourself. Now the table is way more valuable to you than when you bought it an hour ago.

Also, we hate losing. We hate losing much more than we like winning. We will do almost anything to avoid losing. We hate losing so much that sometimes we would rather not love at all than risk loving and losing.

Marketers can use this insight by creating no-lose situations for their customers. Trial subscriptions, money back offers and liberal return policies work. They work because consumers get ownership for a period of time and this makes them feel attached to the product. And of course, it gets them over the initial hesitation in buying.

Creating no-lose situations for consumers seems to increase the risks for the marketers. Perhaps, that is why your CFO is unlikely to be very pleased with you for making the suggestion. It is very difficult to prove to the CFO that consumers will behave irrationally.

Actually the no-lose offer is a win-win offer for the marketer and the consumer. If only we could convince the rationalists about it.

Create Positive Expectations

A few years ago, a book by Rhonda Bryne, *The Secret*, shot to the top of best-seller lists all over the world. The secret of the book was positive expectations. Basically, it said that if you believe something is going to happen, it will happen. Many people believe that Ms. Bryne took the idea to a ridiculous level, but certainly, the basic premise is sound.

She was not the first person to come up with the idea. There have been other books on the subject such as *The Power of Positive Thinking* by Dr Norman Vincent Peale. George Bernard Shaw wrote a play about this called *Pygmalion* that was later turned into a musical and then a movie called My Fair Lady. Psychologists refer to this idea of self-fulfilling expectations as 'The Pygmalion Effect'.

There is a lot of power in the beliefs of human beings. This is the reason why placebos work. There have been numerous scientific experiments to show that placebos can cure people of certain kinds of ailments. In fact, now there is even a hierarchy of placebos. A white coloured pill works, but a blue one works better. And red and white capsules work best of all.

Packaging is the placebo of marketing. The perceived quality of a product depends a lot on its packaging. The same pen when sold in a nice box is more valued than when sold loose. Perfume brands spend more money on packaging than on the product itself.

There are other ways of creating positive expectations. We have already seen the power of smell in creating a better disposition. Price also works as an indicator of high quality. And, of course, positive word of mouth works best of all. If people have told you that a restaurant or a movie is great, then you are less likely to feel that you didn't have a good time.

At Euro RSCG India, we were able to predict the fate of movies before they were released by using this idea. Our insight was that there were some people who were critical in spreading word of mouth opinion. We called these people Prosumers and I will talk more about them in a later chapter. To predict the fate of movies at the box office, we went to Prosumers and checked with them which movies they thought would do well. We found a very high correlation (around 90%) between what Prosumers said would happen to a movie and what actually happened at the box office.

We got a lot of publicity - both positive and negative - for our predictions. But really, people already know whether or not they are going to enjoy a movie BEFORE they see it. All we did was to capture these expectations.

So how can we create positive expectations for our brands? There are no easy formulas, but a combination of packaging, pricing and opinion management should work wonders.

Use Peer Pressure in your Favour

We tend to think of consumers as individuals taking decisions all by themselves. But the reality is that human beings are social animals and consumption is a social event. As marketers, we need to understand how the inter personal dynamics work among consumers.

Dan Ariely found that people order differently in a restaurant when they order privately (by writing down their choices, for example) than when they order publicly by calling out their order to the waiter. Not only did their order change when they ordered publicly, even their satisfaction level with the food changed.

The way it works is as follows. The first person to order can order whatever he likes from the menu. The second person will try to avoid what the first person has ordered and will ask for something from the rest of the menu. The third person will avoid the first two items and so on. The last person to order has the least number of options. The satisfaction level of the people in this group falls with the reduction in the number of options. So only the first person is going to be truly satisfied with his meal. One way to avoid this is to have people write down their orders, so that everyone gets the same number of options.

Sometimes it works the opposite way, though. You may go and enroll in a gym only because everyone in your group is doing so, or have an ice cream because everyone else is having one. There is no hard and fast rule for how the inter personal interactions will affect purchase. The only point to be made is that we need to be aware that buying decisions aren't lonely decisions but often group ones.

Now let us look at some examples of irrational behaviour of consumers.

This Tastes So... White!

A recent trend is for companies to use social causes to promote their brands. We will discuss more on this in a later section. For now, let's focus on a seemingly irrational aspect of human behaviour.

Coca Cola launched a campaign in the USA and Canada in the winter of the year 2011 to help save the habitat of the polar bear. As part of this campaign, they changed their iconic red cans to white.

My son, who studies in Canada, read this article and wrote back to say that he had bought this new white can thinking it was a Diet Coke. Apparently, he was not the only one to have made this mistake. Many other consumers did so too.

But what is even more interesting is that people who drank the Coke from the new white cans, thought it tasted different. They thought it was flat. There was an uproar on social media, which led to Coke back tracking and re-launching a new red can with the polar bear motif .

This is the bit that fascinates me - a change in colour in packaging is enough to make people think that the taste of the product has changed. Need we say more about the power of colour?

If we are to truly get the new marketing, we have to understand that consumers are irrational and we have to study their culture. Well, colour is a manifestation of both these ideas. Colour creates feelings that we aren't able to explain in rational terms. Also, the same colour evokes different feelings in different cultures.

For some irrational and cultural reasons, red and white is the best colour combination to use for a brand. Look at the leading brands in many different categories and you will see that the leader is red and white. Coca Cola is an obvious example, and before Coca Cola, Thums Up had the same colour scheme. Colgate, Airtel, Wills Navy Cut, Lifebuoy, Toyota, and of course, Red & White have all gained from using this colour combination. Sports teams think of it as a good colour scheme to bring them luck. Manchester United, Liverpool and Arsenal have certainly benefitted, though Delhi Daredevils may not be so sure. And let's not forget the Red Cross and the general symbol for medicine.

Red is a great colour in most cultures. In India, it is the colour of marriage and signifies purity. In China, it is the colour of celebration. In Anglo Saxon cultures, it is the colour of passion and love, though it also signifies danger. But red is not universally liked. In South Africa and some other places, red is the colour of mourning. In fact, the Red Cross has changed its colours to green and white in those countries.

White, on the other hand, is all about purity. It is light and mild; so it is a good colour to use in brand extensions to signify a diet, or a milder version of the product. Green is the colour of nature. So it works for brands that are herbal or Ayurvedic.

Having said that, a few brands have benefited by innovating with colours and going against the grain of their category. For example, the dominant colour in banking is blue. We can see this in the logos of HDFC Bank, State Bank of India, Citibank, Bank of America, Standard Chartered Bank, Deutsche Bank, Bank of India, Yes Bank, Indian Bank and Allahabad Bank. That's a long list, but actually, is only a partial one. In this sea of blue, HSBC has always been red and white.

Perhaps, blue signified royalty, while HSBC wanted to be more of a mass brand. Normally, finance people hate the colour red (in their world, profits are black and losses are red).A few years ago, HSBC decided that there was too much red in its logo; they toned it down and increased the white. I wonder if that made any difference to the perceptions of their service.

More recently, Bank of Baroda has changed its colour to a bright orange to go with their sun logo. Let's see how that works for BOB. Maybe consumers will think BOB bankers have a sunnier disposition now.

We have always known that colours affect your mood. But guess what, it might even affect the way consumers perceive your product's taste, service and value.

Smell that Service

"The most primal and evocative of our senses. Smell is the only human sense that brings floating molecules from our environment directly in contact with our neurons." Thus begins a video, *The Power of Smell*, on the World Science Festival website.

Smell does amazing things to us and we don't even realise it. I found a slide show on the Woman's Day website that talks about the effects of different smells on us. There were some obvious ones like coffee that give us a jolt of energy (you just have to smell it, not actually drink it). The most surprising was that cinnamon actually makes you a nicer and kinder person. Geranium helps you get hormonal balance and thus alleviate PMS and menopausal symptoms.

Given the importance of this sense, do you have a 'smell strategy' for your brand? Some categories and brands have begun to use this in interesting ways.

Take real estate in the USA. Houses that are up for sale over there have 'open' days when the owners leave their homes in the care of the real estate agent who shows it to prospective buyers. It has been found that if the house smells good, then it fetches a higher price. So real estate agents advise their clients to bake cinnamon bread or chocolate chip cookies just before leaving on 'open house' days.

BMW has managed to bottle the 'new car' smell and uses it to great advantage. They found that when they sprayed a car that came to the workshop for maintenance with the 'new car' spray, the service ratings on their service went up. BMW has even come out with scratch and sniff ads that have the same smell. It obviously makes people desire a BMW more. Makes quite a difference from just talking about power and torque.

Interestingly, the BMW scratch and sniff ads show a woman in the main visual. It is well known that a woman's sense of smell is more developed than a man's. In fact, scientists believe that women use smell to find their perfect life partner as well.

I love reading books and now prefer reading them as ebooks rather than as physical books. This is a controversial preference, as most people who like books still prefer them in the physical form. My arguments are all rational - you can buy ebooks quickly and easily, you can carry them everywhere, you can change the font sizes to read them more comfortably, you can mark passages and make notes easily. You can even lend some of them. The one argument that always stumps me is the one about smell. People love the smell of books, both new ones and old musty ones. That is part of the pleasure of reading. I agree with that and the sooner ebooks can copy the smell of physical books, the more trees we will save.

Cookie Man is an Australian chain of freshly baked cookies that operates in India. The head of the chain in India, Pattabhi Rama Rao, told me once that his biggest marketing weapon is the smell of freshly baked cookies. That is what draws the customers to the store. To maximize the effectiveness of this weapon, he ensures that his stores are never in a food court since there are already a large number of food smells in that area. He pays a premium to place his stores in general shopping areas, so as to attract the hungry shopper. As a consumer, I can vouch for the effectiveness of his strategy.

A smell-strategy for a food brand sounds obvious. A smell-strategy for real estate or a car brand - not so much. As marketers, we tend to focus on appealing to the consumers' rational brain. To do that, we tend to use words - either spoken or written. The main senses that we use are the eyes and the ears. But we do have three other senses and we need to use them too.

If we like the smell of money, then we need to have a smell-strategy for our brands.

You Smell Different

Howard Schulz, the CEO and chairman of Starbucks, started working at Starbucks on my birthday in the year 1982. Perhaps, that is the reason why I have a special affinity for the brand Starbucks. (That, my love for coffee and my egoistical desire to be regarded as a connoisseur). However, this story is not about me, but about the smell of a Starbucks coffee shop.

Howard Schulz got the idea of opening coffee bars in the United States when he was on a visit to Italy. While there, he explored espresso bars in Milan and Verona, and observed the power of coffee in connecting people and creating a sense of community among them. He resolved to bring world class coffee and the romance of Italian espresso bars to the United States.

At that time, Americans drank a lot of coffee, but they weren't too particular about its quality. The typical American diner would have a pot of coffee brewing all through the day and customers would get unlimited amounts of the dark liquid. Coffee had a functional purpose - to wake you up - and nobody cared for it beyond that.

Mr. Schulz turned Americans into coffee connoisseurs. Everyone developed their own particular way in which they liked their coffee. If you Google the words 'How to order at Starbucks' (within quotes), you will get over 189,000 results with the exact match. Some of the ways in which people order their coffee are really bizarre and elaborate. Truly, Starbucks turned blasé Americans into coffee aficionados - extremely particular about how exactly their coffee was made and served.

As an aside, do you know the longest Starbucks order ever? It is: Double Ristretto Venti Half-Soy Nonfat Decaf Organic Chocolate Brownie Iced Vanilla Double-Shot Gingerbread Frappuccino Extra Hot With Foam Whipped Cream Upside Down Double Blended, One Sweet' N Low and One Nutrasweet, and Ice.

It was ordered in December 1997 in a small Starbucks in a small Montana town. It was finally made and delivered in October 1998, exactly one day after the death of the man who had ordered it.

The point about all this is that Starbucks was supposed to be all about coffee. When you entered a store, you smelt the coffee. You saw the baristas make the coffee. You could buy coffee accessories. Sure you could buy some food and some music, but the essential thing about Starbucks was coffee.

Then Starbucks decided to sell breakfast.

It seemed to make perfect sense. Most Americans would buy a Starbucks coffee on their way to work. They would also buy a breakfast sandwich either before or after buying their coffee. So it made sense for Starbucks to start selling both and make consumers happy.

The sandwich which Starbucks sold had to be heated in an oven. Heating it caused the cheese to melt and the smell of the cheese spread through the store. Now Starbucks didn't just smell of the coffee, it also smelt of cheese.

The problem is that by then other restaurant chains had started to improve the quality of the coffee that they served. All these chains, like McDonalds, served food with cheese as well. So they smelt of cheese anyway. Now Starbucks smelt like them.

The coffee at Starbucks was much better than the coffee at McDonalds, but now people weren't so sure. Their noses were confused. Had Starbucks changed the quality of the coffee?

All this happened in the period when Howard Schulz had stepped down from his post as ceo (all designations in Starbucks are written without capitals). In his book, Onward, Mr. Schultz says he was troubled by this move, but decided not to interfere.

Until he got back to the job in the year 2008.

By then, breakfast contributed a significant part of the revenues at Starbucks. The company itself was doing badly. In fact, the day that Starbucks announced its worst ever financial results was also the day it announced that it was no longer going to sell breakfast sandwiches.

That takes some guts. To cut out a big revenue earner at a time when revenues are down. Yet, Howard Schulz strongly believed that if Starbucks was going to go back to capture its original position of the best coffee in town, then it had to focus on coffee and nothing else.

The story has a happy ending, of course. Mr. Schulz created a turnaround at his company by doing a bunch of different things. But an important element in his new strategy was making his stores smell of coffee again.

By the way, Starbucks did reintroduce breakfast sandwiches later. By then, the engineers in the company had figured out a way of heating the sandwiches without making the stores smell of cheese. Only then did their boss relent.

No wonder they say that a good boss has to have a strong sense of smell.

The Sound of your Brand

How do you feel when the national anthem is played? How did our freedom fighters feel when they sang 'Vande Mataram'? What mood do you get into when you hear the sound of temple bells or the Adhan (the Muslim call to prayer)? Do you start day-dreaming when you hear the sound of the Harley Davidson engine?

Countries and religions have always used sound to brand themselves. All countries have a national anthem to go with their national flag. India has a national song in addition to our national anthem. Each major religion has well defined sounds. Hindusim has the sound of Om, the temple bells, the blowing of the conch and the bhajans. Churches have bells and choirs. Buddhism has its chants. Islam has its melodic calls to prayer. Plus there is sufi music from a sect of Muslims.

Armies have their battle cries. The rugby team of New Zealand does the 'haka' before each match, which is an indigenous war dance and song. It sends shivers down the spine of the opposition, while also firing up the Kiwi team and their supporters.

Daniel Jackson, one of the gurus of Sonic branding, says: "Sound conveys the emotion while the pictures convey the information." The strongest brands in the world have very well defined sounds. We are all familiar with the Intel 'Bong', the Britannia signature and the Titan music (which is from the Third Movement of Mozart's 25th Symphony).

Each of these signature sounds not only remind us of the brand, but also of the emotions we feel when we encounter the brand. Most people from my generation have probably not heard the Doordarshan signature tune for years. Yet, when we do hear it, it once again evokes the joy and excitement that we felt when we first watched television. We know these songs instantly even if we are not musically inclined and can't sing or hum a tune.

The best brands go much beyond having signature sounds in their advertising. They evolve a consistent palette of sounds that consumers hear across all touch points. In his book, Mr Jackson has a case study on how BMW really fusses over every sound that their cars make.

"Every sound made by a BMW is analysed by a team of over two hundred acoustic engineers to ensure they are both mechanically and aesthetically correct. The doors have a reassuringly solid sound as they close, the buttons click with purpose and the dashboard remains silent whatever the driving conditions. Then, of course, there is the main sound producer, the engine. BMW has to live up to the fact that it is known as a luxury sports saloon manufacturer. It has to be ensured that the cars sound sporty while keeping engine noise to a desirable level. Achieving this balance is both complex and expensive; but if the brand experience is to be right, the expense is well worth it.

The importance of sound in cars can really be understood when sound is absent. Recently, my son had the opportunity to test drive Tesla's Model S. The Model S calls itself 'the world's first premium electric sedan'. It is a really powerful car that can instantly reach full power, unlike petrol cars whose engines need to rev up to full power. As a result, the Model S leaves other cars way behind when it starts off from signal lights. My son enjoyed driving the car very much but ended up saying that he would rather buy a BMW since he missed the roar of the engine. Electric cars are worried about this issue and are experimenting with creating sounds to artificially fill the emptiness that people feel while driving them.

Given the importance of sounds, it is really important that brands define and maintain their own sounds. Mr. Jackson is distressed by brands that buy the rights to popular music tracks. He says: "Pepsi has always sponsored the music of others. In many ways, Pepsi helped make Madonna famous, as they did Boyzone and Hear'say in the UK (thanks Pepsi). Coke, however, made itself famous through its creation of music rather than endorsement of it." He is talking here of the famous Coke song created in the early seventies: "I'd like to buy the world a Coke."

With the growth of technology, brands have more touch points where they can be 'heard'. Ring tones, caller tunes, IVRs and the hold music are four touch points on the phone. Plus, there are mass media vehicles, retail channels and so on.

The sound doesn't need to be exactly the same everywhere, but needs to come from the same palette so that it is recognised as belonging to the brand. Titan uses its tune in so many different ways. They sing it, play it and hum it - and all this at different tempos! Even though the original piece of music wasn't known to most Indians, it has stuck in all our heads and we are reminded of Titan and the joy of gifting every time we hear it.

Isn't that what all brands dream to achieve?

The Most Powerful Brands in the World

Can you name the country that each monument above is associated with?

Most people find that fairly easy to do. Maybe you will get stuck with one or two monuments, but for the most part, the name of the country pops into your head as soon as you see the monument.

Can you name the religion to which each symbol on the next page corresponds? I found this a little tougher, but I got the major religions right.

Countries and religions are the most powerful brands in the world. Most people identify themselves by the country they belong to and/or the religion they are affiliated with. Brands provide a sense of identity to people, and by that yardstick, these are really strong brands.

So what can regular brands learn from these super strong brands? Martin Lindstrom, who has done a lot of work in the area of neural marketing, has identified ten commandments or lessons that brands can learn from religion. I found these really fascinating, so here is Mr. Lindstrom's complete list - though the explanation and comments are mine.

1. A sense of belonging: Brands are about belonging to a community. For example, Mac users feel a sense of kinship towards each other as do Harley Davidson owners. At other times, brands try to align themselves with pre-existing communities like Nike tries to be part of the community of athletes.

2. A clear vision: Each strong brand stands for something. Nike is about doing the best that you can physically. Apple is about user friendly design. Starbucks makes you feel like a connoisseur.

3. Power from the enemy: Strong brands have a clearly defined enemy. Just like the good and evil stories that all religions have, brands too need a villain to improve the halo around themselves. So Coke has Pepsi and Apple has Microsoft (and maybe Google). In some cases, the enemy may not be a brand. So The Body Shop's enemy is the idea of big businesses that harm society and the environment.

4. Authenticity: Mr. Lindstrom says there are four defining components of authenticity - it's real, it's relevant, it has rituals and is part of a story. If the brand feels fake, then obviously, it will not have too many followers.

5. Consistency: Routines and habits help create brand loyalty. Oreo is a cream biscuit that Americans eat with milk. It has become a ritual such that they can't have milk without Oreos. Similarly, there are set ways in which you have certain kinds of drinks - tequila and Corona beer for example. Newspapers become a habit quite quickly and have proven quite difficult to shake off.

6. Perfection: The strongest brands are usually the best in their category. They excel in the area that they are known for. It could be low price for Walmart or punctuality for Indigo Airlines.

7. Symbols: This is where brands really need to learn from religions. Religions have so many symbols - the cross, the crescent flag, the Star of David and so on. The priests wear certain kind of clothes. Many religions are associated with a certain kind of colour, a certain language and even a way of greeting other members of the community. Brands are acquiring more and more symbols too. Lady Gaga and her 'little monster' fans have their own hand gestures, tattoos and so on.

8. Mystery: Only Parsi males can enter a Parsi fire temple. The rituals of the Freemasons are closed to all outsiders. These mysteries help to make these religions more attractive. Similarly, KFC's eleven secret spices and the Coca-Cola recipe help create mystique around those brands. Even controversies around how Netflix started or who did what at Twitter help the respective brands.

9. Rituals: This is linked to point number five about consistency. Brand rituals are becoming important as marketing becomes more experiential. Other rituals include the flame of the Olympics and the chants of football teams.

10. Sensory appeal: Religions appeal to all our senses. Incense sticks tickle our noses. The bells, the singing and the chants work on our ears. The symbols are there for us to see. Being part of a religion is really about a way of life. Brands try to be that too. Is there a Nike way of life? An Apple way of life?

They say that cricket and movies are like religion in India. That means that they are a way of life for millions of people here. Similarly, brands try to become a way of life. A philosophy of life. That goes beyond the mere rational benefit that the product offers. In fact, while on the subject, what exactly is the rational promise of a religion?

Pricing Mysteries that will Make your Head Itch

Long, long time ago, when the price of petrol was INR 35 per litre, the oil marketing companies in India were allowed to launch value added fuels. Each major company in India promptly did so. Bharat Petroleum launched Speed, Indian Oil launched Xtra and Hindustan Petroleum launched Power.

These premium fuels typically charged an additional INR 2.50 per litre, or 7% more expensive than ordinary petrol.

The new brands were backed up with lots of advertising support and soon about a quarter of all motorists were using these premium fuels in their vehicles.

That was then. Today, the price of petrol has gone up to INR 75 per litre.

The premium for the value added fuels is still INR 2.5 per litre. Now premium fuels are only 3% more expensive than regular petrol. Yet, the share of premium fuel sales has gone down from 25% to less than 8% and continues to fall.

Doesn't make sense, does it?

Let's look at another example. The detergent powders market in India used to be divided into two parts: the premium full-blown powders like Surf and the discount powders like Nirma. The latter was the bigger market - more than ten times the size of the premium market. Of course, it helped that Nirma was one-third the price of Surf.

Then along came Ariel (and later other concentrate powders), priced at three times the price of the premium powders. Now consumers had to chose between three very different price points. You would imagine that the cheapest segment of the market would be the largest, but you couldn't be more wrong. Nearly half the market has now moved up to the middle segment of the premium detergent powders.

Have you heard about mail-in rebates? This is where you buy a product at its sticker price, but then you send a proof of purchase to the manufacturer and in return you get a refund of part or full of what you have paid by cheque. This seems strange for two reasons. If you want to give a discount, why do it in this complicated way? Also, some of the discounts are huge - in one case it was 100% of the sticker price. Why would you want to sell a product for free?

Mail-in rebates sound great on point of sale material, but are quite difficult for consumers to actually redeem. A large percentage of consumers forget to mail the vouchers and thus the company has to pay out much less than what appears. This is classical irrational behaviour - a consumer buys a product because of a promised discount, but then forgets to actually claim it.

Talking of sticker prices, do you remember the Bata pricing? Bata used to price all their products just 1 paise short of the rupee. Thus, INR 99.99 rather than INR100. You would think that consumers would see through this and understand that it basically costs one hundred rupees. But, no! Consumers still fall for this trick after all these years.

Traditionally, marketers don't seem to have given sufficient attention to pricing. A lot of creativity can go into pricing which can help sales and, sometimes, even help build the brand or the category. This is slowly beginning to happen as our next chapter illustrates.

How to Make Money by Selling for Free

Business is all about making money. It makes no sense to give away your product for free. Yet, many internet services seem to be doing just that. And these companies are not going bankrupt but getting mind boggling valuations. So how do companies make money by selling for free?

Let me start with the story of two Harvard graduates, Yifan Zhang and Geoff Oberhofer. They studied Behavioral Economics in their course and were inspired to base their business model on one of the principles of this new science.

They have started a business that they call Gym-pact. Their offer is simple. Gym-pact asks you to make a minimum commitment about how often you will use the gym. Suppose you commit to using the gym at least once a week; you pay nothing so long as you come there at least once a week. But if you don't show up at least once a week, then you will be charged a penalty for that week. Don't show up the next week either and you will pay another penalty and so on.

Their stated mission is that they want to help you stay fit. Working out in the gym is the classical case where you lose something in the present (the trouble of waking up early, going to the gym, the pain of the workout), so that you gain something in the future (lose weight, look good, stay healthy). The problem is that we much prefer present gain to future benefits. So we will always find excuses to not go to the gym and let the future take care of itself. Gym-pact attempts to give you a benefit in the present for going to the gym (you save money) and also helps you gain in the future.

Isn't this a brilliant use of pricing as a marketing tool? We all know that when we sign up for the gym, we are determined to go there everyday. But soon our resolve weakens and we stop going. Gym-pact banks on this insight into human nature to make money. The beauty of the scheme is that the pricing strategy helps to build the brand even as it makes money for the owners.

This raises the issue about why we don't use price more aggressively. Most marketers take price as a given - something that is determined by the finance people. Usually, price is determined by taking costs and adding on a profit margin. The only variation is when we offer discounts to customers

Chris Anderson is the editor in chief of the *Wired* magazine and has written a book called *Free*. In the book, he argues that one of the big changes in the new economy is that consumers are used to getting a lot of stuff for free. Businesses, however, still need to make money. Several industries have evolved models where they make money even though some of their products/services are given away for free. Mr. Anderson outlines several such examples in his book. By the way, his book can be downloaded for free as an unabridged audio book from here (http://goo.gl/yKJ9). However, if you want a physical copy, then, of course, you need to buy it. A classical case of giving something for free and charging for something else.

Musicians are doing that now. Some of them give away their music for free on their websites and then make money from concerts and merchandise. Not long ago, it used to be that concerts and merchandise were marketing tools for promoting the CDs. How things have changed.

Stop press: Did you read that Amazon has priced its new Kindle tablet so aggressively that it is likely to lose USD 50 per piece? They plan to sell millions, which means the losses aren't going to be small. But they are taking the larger view and see this discount as a way of promoting their brand and gaining long-term customers. They will make money by selling books, music and movies to this customer.

Do you know of other examples of innovative uses of price as a marketing tool? Or do you have ideas on how an industry could use price more creatively? I would love to hear of them.

Guru-Speak: Everything is Going to be Free

The most fascinating aspect of Chris Anderson's book, *Free*, is the sidebars. Here he gives a series of examples from different industries on how they can sell for free. Here are a few of them:

How Can Air Travel be Free?

Discount airlines do have lower costs than full fare airlines. However, the difference in price is starker than the difference in costs. How do they manage? Turns out that discount airlines have some surprising sources of revenue:

- Cancellations and date changes: This is often the second highest source of revenue. People buy cheap tickets in advance and then have to cancel or change them. This costs a lot of money.
- Food sales on board.
- Price for special seats and extra bags.
- Price for priority boarding and faster retrieval of bags.
- Advertising revenue from brands who want to reach your customers.

How can a DVR be Free?

Satellite TV companies like Tata Sky and Comcast often give away the digital video recorders almost for free. They are able to recover the money through installation fees, their monthly subscription for the TV and by selling other services.

How can Everything in a Store be Free?

Sample Lab is a boutique in Tokyo that gives its customers up to five free items every time they visit. This store has huge traffic and has become very fashionable. It makes money by charging membership fees from customers, charging a rental for shelves from brands and charging for feedback from customers.

How can a Textbook be Free?

As a parent of a college-going son, I know how exorbitant it is to buy text books in the USA and Canada. Mr. Anderson suggests that one way around this would be to open up the content of textbooks and offer students the option of browsing books online for free, or buying an individual chapter if they require. A whole menu of options can be created depending on whether the students want the whole book or an individual chapter, or whether they want the content online as PDF or a printed-on-demand copy.

The idea behind this is to have more students buying the products to make up in volume what you lose in margins. Also, it may attract more authors since the total royalty they get can be higher than what they get in the standard textbook model.

How Can University Education be Free?

Recently, there has been a growth of Massive Online Open Courses (MOOC) like Coursera. I did a course on gamification there that was taught by a Wharton Professor. The course was professionally conducted, had great content and was a good learning experience. Each lesson was a video that was punctuated with multiple-choice questions to check comprehension. There were quizzes and exams to be taken and assignments to be submitted for evaluation. All this was for free. There was even a certificate of completion at the end, though, that had to be paid for.

Coursera is a for-profit company. It generates revenue through certification fees, introducing students to potential employers and recruiters (with student consent), tutoring, sponsorships and tuition fees. The teachers use the opportunity to sell books and get on lecture tours.

I didn't pay for my course since I wasn't interested in the certificate, but I did buy my Professor's book.

Brand Rituals Unplugged

Marketers love rituals around their brands. Corona beer is always drunk from the bottle with a wedge of lime stuck in the neck. Everyone breaks a Kit Kat by sliding a finger down the ridge. And tequila has its own unique ceremony for drinking it.

Once we see a new and shiny technique that works, we all want to replicate it for our brands. So Pepsi tries to teach you to hold their cans in a certain (elegant? clumsy?) way. And now Oreo wants you to eat it with a 'twist, lick and dunk'.

The film is likeable. But do we expect a lot of people to start eating Oreos in this way? Do we seriously expect children to shake their hips after they have their Horlicks? Should we keep inventing newer (and more bizarre) brand rituals?

My sense is that brand rituals need to be discovered, not invented. The best ones are based on a cultural truth. Someone discovers a few consumers performing the ritual and makes it popular. It's pretty optimistic to invent a ritual from scratch and expect it to catch on.

The Oreo ritual probably comes from a cultural insight in the USA. Perhaps kids there do dunk their cookies in milk. That was the insight of the famous 'Got milk' campaign too. But in India, children don't do that. Grown-ups dunk salty biscuits into their tea in India, but do kids dunk sweet biscuits?

Similarly, the famous 'Whatsup?' campaign from Budweiser was based on a cultural discovery. The agency discovered that people actually greeted each other that way. They then made the phrase famous.

I am sure you can think of many brands that are trying to tie their brands to a ritual. I'd love to hear which of them you think are tied to a cultural truth and which are just force fits. The other question I have is whether rituals only work for food and drink brands. Are there any other brands that have brand rituals?

The Schizophrenic Marketer

This section has been about the irrational consumer. It's a long section with many pieces in it. It could probably be longer as marketers keep discovering new insights into why consumers really buy their brands. But let's pause here and discuss a mindset issue and an ethical one at that.

Marketing people know that consumers are driven by irrational desires. They nod knowingly when they come across case studies like the ones in this section of the book. And yet, when they get into decision making mode on their own brands, they behave as if consumers are totally rational. I have called this piece *The Schizophrenic Marketer*, but I might as well have called it *The Irrational Marketer*.

In a board room, it is easier to make the assumption that the consumer is rational. If the consumer is rational and is seeking the best value, then we just have to let them know that our product provides slightly better value and they will buy it. That sounds easy to do and we build our strategies around that idea.

Except, of course, that consumers don't behave like that. The marketing battlefield is littered with the corpses of brands that were actually better value than their more successful competitors, but just didn't become a hit with consumers.

Understanding irrational insights into how consumers behave is messy. The science of behavioural economics is quite new and the tenets are still evolving. We take decisions with our rational mind and that part of our brain still can't fully accept that the irrational part is stronger. Hence, there is a struggle between the rational part of our brain and the rest. And often, the rational part wins, in spite of the evidence.

There is also the question of ethics. Are we manipulating our customers when we appeal to the irrational? Is it somehow unethical to use irrational insights and more gentlemanly to just provide better value to consumers and let them decide?

My argument rests on the idea of marketing itself. Marketing is the function, which tries to understand the needs of the customer and provides a product or service to fulfil it. If that is so, then isn't it the duty of the marketer to really understand the true reasons why a customer buys and not just find the most convenient reasons? To me, the irrational insights are the true insights and the rational ones are often the superficial insights.

The problem is in the label. So long as we call it irrational, it sounds wrong. Irrational is a negative word. Perhaps, we need a more positive label. Something like 'primary' insights. Then the rational insights would be called secondary or tertiary insights. Perhaps, then we would start to look deeper. We would consider it lazy to build a strategy only on the basis of secondary insights.

That's really what it boils down to then. Working with only rational insights is lazy, while understanding the irrational reasons is thorough. Now are you convinced that this is the way forward?

Guru-speak: Buy-ology

The problem with behavioural economics is that it is about the irrational. It does not appeal to our rational side, and hence, we don't believe it. How do economists convince themselves and the rest of us, that their conclusions are real and not just interesting theories?

One way is to study what happens in our brains. That is precisely what neuro-marketing experts have been doing. One of the leaders in this field is Martin Lindstrom.

Mr. Lindstrom has done what he calls the largest neuro-marketing study ever. He used technologies like fMRI and electroencephalogram to see inside the brains of his respondents, and see exactly what happened there when they saw, smelt, heard or felt something. For the first time, marketers can truly understand the effects of their work. Marketers no longer need to ask questions of consumers or deduce the effects from observing their behaviour. They can now 'see' what actually happens. The following chapter captures some of the conclusions and recommendations of Mr. Lindstrom.

Create A 'Smashable' Brand Identity

In the year 1915, Coca Cola briefed a designer to create a bottle that was recognisable even if it was smashed into a hundred pieces. Martin Lindstrom tells this story to illustrate the importance of creating brand properties beyond just the logo. Such 'smashable' brand identity could be a symbol, colour, shape, smell etc.

In the case of Coca Cola, there are several properties that remind us of the brand even when we don't see the logo. This includes the colour red, the sound of a can opening, the tinkle of ice, the sound of the liquid being poured and so on. By careful repetition and association, Coke has managed to appropriate all these properties.

Similarly, the swoosh reminds us of Nike, the layout of the white search page reminds us of Google, the shape of an individual piece reminds of Lego toys, the profile of a cowboy makes people think of Marlboro and so on.

Focus on Emotional/Irrational Appeals

Alfred Hitchcock always had two scripts for every movie that he made. There was the blue script that set out in detail what was to happen on screen - the lines that the actors had to speak, the way they had to move, the props that were required, the instructions for lighting and so on. He also had a secret green script that set out exactly what emotions he wanted the audience to have at each moment in the film. This script was all about how to create those emotions in the viewers.

The main thrust of Mr. Lindstrom's argument is that marketers should focus more on the emotional or irrational brand appeal rather than the rational one. He recommends that each brand must create its own green script for each touch point and each piece of communication.

How to Create a Social Campaign

In his books and talks, Mr. Lindstrom talks about the importance of word of mouth. He suggests that a brand needs to go through the phases of seeding, incubating and adoption. The ratio of people who need to be reached is 1:9:90. In other words, seed with one, incubate with nine and get adoption with ninety.

One of his more interesting conclusions is that the incubation period needs to be as long as nine months. He suggests that it takes that long for word of mouth about a brand to get around. He presents data that suggests that adoption doubles when a brand seeds for six months compared to seeding for three months and doubles once again when seeded for nine.

Mr. Lindstrom suggests a four stage approach to seeding and incubation:

- Revelation: This is about suggesting something amazing in the product. Like a lifetime guarantee or a unique origin. Something that can form the basis for the buzz. For Hendricks Gin, the revelation was that is was really old - one hundred and twenty six years old and available only to select customers in a few select bars.

- A-ha Moment: This is all about staging the brand such that people start saying, "Have you heard?" For Hendricks Gin, this was done by serving the gin with great ceremony to glamorous customers. The Gin was served from a teapot into tea cups which had wine glass stems (cupglasses). That got people talking and wondering about the brand.

- Tipping Point: This is where the conversation moves from 'just' an interesting conversation to a brand conversation. This is where you are telling the brand story to the nine people who are going to spread the word to ninety people.

- Show off: In order for an insider conversation to become widespread, you need some way for the insiders to 'show off' their status. This could be a wristband like it was for Livestrong, or it could be the cup-glass for Hendricks. Something that others can notice and ask questions about.

Aspiration Group

One of the mantras of the new marketing thinking is that brands need to focus on a core audience who in turn will spread the word. Elsewhere in this book, I refer to them as Prosumers. Mr. Lindstrom calls them the aspiration group. Each strong brand seems to focus only on their aspiration group and the rest of the audience aspires to be like those in the group.

For Nike, the aspiration group is athletes. For Apple, it is designers. For Red Bull, it is extreme sports enthusiasts.

Somatic Markers

Elsewhere in this book, I refer to the idea of creating memorable experiences for customers. Mr. Lindstrom has an interesting term for these. He calls them somatic markers. These are unforgettable emotional bookmarks that remind you of the experience you had when you first encountered the brand.

Whole countries may share somatic markers. For example, people all over the world remember where they were and what they were doing when the planes hit the World Trade Centre in New York on September 11, 2001. Whole countries remember the day when a beloved leader dies - JFK or Gandhi for example. The challenge is to create a somatic marker for brands.

Red Bull certainly succeeded in creating a somatic marker with Felix Baumgartner's jump from space. Similarly, Steve Jobs created one by taking the Macbook Air out of an envelope. The announcement by Jeff Bezos that Amazon will use drones to deliver its packages may prove to be another somatic marker.

ELEPHANT IN THE ROOM:

CONSUMERS HATE MAKING CHOICES

Choose - Do you Like Choice or you Don't?

Heard the one about the man who went to a restaurant and asked for a Coke? Here is how the conversation went:

Customer: May I have a Coke, please?
Waiter: Sure, Sir. Would that be a regular Coke or a diet Coke?
C: Regular, please.
W: Sure. Would you like a Coke Classic, Cherry Coke or Caffeine Free Coke? Or perhaps you would like a Vanilla Coke or Coke with Lime? We also have Coke Zero and Coke Light. With or without Splenda?
C: I think I will just have a coffee.
W: Sure Sir. What kind of coffee would you like?...

Today we have more categories of things, more brands within a category and more options within a brand.

That sounds like a good thing but doesn't always seem to be so. Often people are conflicted by so much choice and get scared. They end up not choosing at all.

Prof. Sheena Iyenger of Columbia University has done a lot of work on this subject and written a fascinating book, *The Art of Choosing*. Her basic thesis is that people tend to get choice-paralysis when confronted with more than six choices at a time.

Prof. Iyenger and her team did the famous jam test to show this. In a California gourmet super market, they set up a tasting table. At certain times they had twenty four bottles of jam open on the table, while at others they had only six bottles available for tasting. Everyone who stopped to taste would get a coupon to buy jam at a discount from the actual aisles where there were dozens of more choices.

What the team found was that 60% of customers stopped when there were more jams on offer and the traffic was 40% when fewer jams were available. However, of the people who stopped at the smaller table, 30% ended up buying a jam, while only 3% of those who stopped at the larger table bought.

More choice attracts people, but then also paralyses them into inaction. Less choice attracts fewer people, but then ends up creating a much larger sale than the larger choice. In the case of the jams, sales were six times more when consumers were given the smaller choice.

This choice-paralysis is also seen in situations which are much more important for people than buying a bottle of jam. Another example given in Iyengar's book is that of pension schemes in the USA (also known as the 401K schemes). The way they operate is that consumers need to choose one fund to manage their pension. In some companies, employees have a choice of only two funds, but this choice goes up to fifty nine options in other firms. You can see where this is going. It is obviously better for everyone to have a pension scheme rather than not having one. And yet, there is a sharp negative correlation between the number of choices on offer and the number of people who opt for any one of them.

So what should marketers do about this? Prof. Iyenger suggests that we evolve strategies to help consumers cope with this extra choice. One way is to create categories. Let people choose between categories. Having made the choice, they can then choose sub categories within the option chosen and so on until they arrive at the final choice. The idea is to give people six choices or less at every stage. And even when we do this, we need to go from simple decisions (fewer choices) to more complex ones.

Of course, before we start categorizing, it would help if marketers cut away extraneous options from their offering. We need to ensure that the choices we offer are distinct and concrete. They need to be real choices.

Else the consumer will just ask for coffee.

Dictatorship and Choice

Steve Jobs was a dictator. By all accounts, he was not one who liked to have a lot of discussion around his decisions. Nor did he believe in consumer research. He just decided what the consumer would like, based on what he liked. And guess what, consumers just lapped up his products even when they weren't the best products in the market.

When Steve Jobs returned to Apple, he found that the company sold twenty three different product lines. He famously made a two by two matrix, put one product in each square, and eliminated all others.

He went one step further.

A lot of computers are bought by corporates and their IT managers usually have their own peculiar specifications. In particular, they like to specify the number and kinds of ports they would like. So IT managers like to insist on a certain number of USB ports, DVD drives, SD/micro SD slots and so on. Most computer manufacturers obey these instructions and end up adding all these ports to all their computers so that they can confirm to all tenders floated. The result is that computers get bloated and are bulkier than their designers would have liked them to be.

Steve Jobs didn't like being dictated to. So he refused to put in any kind of legacy ports. Heck, he would often leave out ports that were not out of date yet, and insist that the world was moving towards another era. The result is that Apple has missed out on the entire institutional segment. Apple computers have remained in their own niche. Loved by the faithfuls, but never quite mainstream.

Lets return to the simplicity of the Apple line up of products. Even today, Apple's range of choices is so simple that it fits on one horizontal bar on their website:

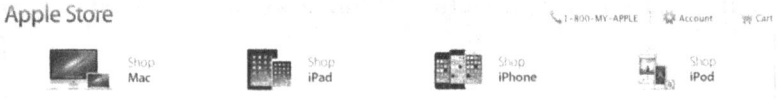

Consumers need to choose between the four lines of products. When you chose a line, you are offered more choices, but the choice is never very wide. It is easy to decide which Apple phone you want. The big decisions there have to do with the choice of colour and the amount of memory.

In contrast, Samsung is a sound marketing company. It does a lot of consumer research and finds out what people want. It is democratic to the extent that it is the only major phone manufacturer that offers smart phones with three different operating systems - Android, Windows Mobile and its own OS Bada relaunched as Tizen.

Samsung has understood that people have individual needs and tries to address as many of them as it can. So it has dozens of options in phones. Some of their phone models are so similar to each other that even their dealers are unable to coherently explain the differences between them. The only difference seems to be in the price. On that they do very well. No matter what you want to spend, chances are that there is a Samsung phone that just fits your budget.

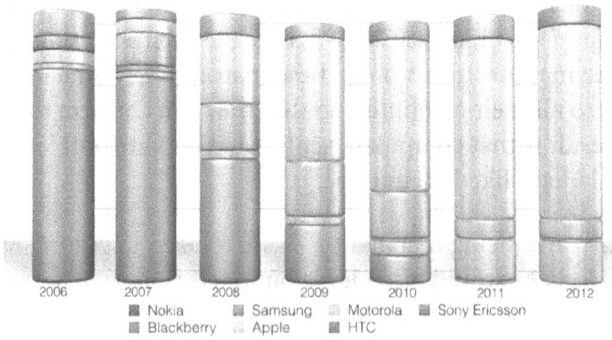

One would think that this large choice would make consumers really happy. And it is true that consumers have been buying a lot of Samsung phones. Samsung is the volume leader in mobile phones in India and all over the world.

The key difference, however, is in profits. Samsung is the volume leader, but Apple is the profit leader. Apple leads over the others by several sack loads of money. See the chart. It shows the share of profits of different phone companies in the years immediately after the launch of the iPhone. Notice the contrasting fortunes of Nokia and the Apple. Notice also the strategy of Samsung - which has grown in volume without growing to the same extent in profits.

This, then, is the effect of offering too much choice. You risk getting the consumer totally confused. And not doing anything as a result.

Choice is a fundamental feature of democracy. But, perhaps, a little bit of dictatorship is good in marketing.

The Joys and Sorrows of the Infinite Scroll

When you search for something on Google, ten results show up on the first page. Turns out that 94% of people are satisfied with those ten results and don't bother going onto the next page.

Social media companies have looked at this tendency of consumers to not go beyond the first page and decided to offer them a never ending first page. As you approach the bottom of the page, more data gets loaded. So whether it is Facebook or Pinterest or Twitter, you keep getting more content as you scroll down.

It is human nature to want to get to the bottom of things. We hate not knowing what exactly we are missing. No wonder, we waste so much time on social media.

Many e-commerce companies have looked at this behavioural trait and decided to offer their entire product range on the first page. This phenomenon of the infinite scroll is having predictable results. As consumers keep scrolling down to look at the choices that they have, they keep getting more and more choices. So they keep scrolling and never actually make a choice. The few people who do click on a product, find that when they hit the back button, they end up at the beginning of the page rather than the place they last were. So the web sites actually penalise you for going away from the page with the infinite scroll.

This has put the e-commerce companies in a bind. On one hand, they want to offer consumers a wider choice. On the other hand, they would like to actually sell some products, not just have consumers look at them. What is the solution?

For the solution, let us turn to the real world. Let's follow some women buying saris. Women don't feel called upon to take a decision on which sari to buy until they have been to at least half a dozen stores and have seen dozens of saris in each store.

The reason for visiting different stores is to arrive at the store that offers them the best collection at the best price. In the selected store, they then settle down to really make their selection. Dozens of saris are opened, creating a small mountain by the end of each customer's journey. As the saris are shown by the salesperson, the customer creates a shortlist. She pulls saris out of the mountain and puts them aside. The shortlist is visited frequently - more saris are added to it and some are removed. Opinions are asked from accompanying family members or friends. The shortlisted saris may be draped on the salesman, a mannequin or even on the customer herself. And then finally, if the shopkeeper is lucky, a decision is made.

The infinite scroll does not allow for shortlisting. If it does allow for shortlisting, it does not allow for the shortlisted products to be viewed in a nice way. And it often does not allow for the shortlist to be shared with friends for their opinion.

This is like a sari shopper being served by a cranky salesperson. The salesperson has an unlimited range of saris and he keeps putting fresh ones on the table in front of the customer. But he does not allow her to take any out of the pile unless she has actually made a decision to buy. If she selects one and then decides not to buy it, then she has to start seeing the saris from the first one onwards - not from the last seen sari.

E-commerce companies are making it difficult for consumers to choose. They are behaving like cranky salesmen. Clearly, the solution lies in having a way to make it easier for customers to choose. Perhaps, a method for short listing would help. The customer needs to be able to view and modify the shortlist easily, share it with friends and make new lists altogether.

Shopping tends to be a messy business. That is why it is fun. Shopping online is too linear and straitjacketed. Perhaps, that is why fewer women shop online.

Why do People have Trademark Outfits?

1998   1999   2001   2004   2005   2007   2008   2009   2010

Steve Jobs was always to be seen in his 'trademark black turtleneck, jeans and sneakers'. One of my ex-bosses always wore a black suit with a white shirt and a black tie to work. I know of people who wear a kurta and jeans everyday. An acquaintance told me that she only wears black outfits.

Have you ever wondered why people fall into this habit? Don't they find it boring to wear the same clothes day after day? Do they miss getting compliments from people they meet on how well dressed they look on a particular day? Do they even know what it is to get complimented for your dressing sense?

Think why they do this. Could it be because they hate taking decisions? It must be so easy to shop for clothes and to decide what to wear each morning if every outfit was the same. Is that why people fall into the habit of wearing the same kind of clothes everyday?

This illustrates what a big pain it is to have to choose and to what lengths people are willing to go to avoid having to make a choice.

Steve Jobs' t-shirts were made by designer Issey Miyake. His jeans were always Levis 501. He mostly wore New Balance sneakers. It is wonderful for these brands to have such loyal customers. Wouldn't all brands like to have such loyal customers?

Brands benefit consumers by reducing the need to constantly make choices.

Choosing the brand for the first time may be difficult. But having done so once, customers don't need to go through the pain again, so long as the brands deliver.

Brands have to perform the balancing act between being totally predictable for the loyal customers and being new and exciting to attract new customers. If they try to be too new, then existing customers will find their familiar products missing and will be forced to choose from the new range. In that case, there is no benefit for them to stay with the brand.

Perhaps, this explains why consumers were so upset when Coke changed its formulation. The old familiar product was gone and now they had to take a decision again. Who knew that consumers hated choice so much?

ELEPHANT IN THE ROOM:

ALL CONSUMERS ARE NOT EQUAL

Hot Air Disrupts

On September 21, 1995, a man in New Delhi dreamt that Lord Ganesha was asking for some milk. So he woke up before dawn and went down to the local temple and convinced the priest to allow him to offer the idol a spoonful of milk. To the surprise of both men, the idol drank up the milk.

The news spread fast. By mid-morning, news had spread all over India. By noon, Hindus in Britain, Canada, Dubai, Nepal and the USA knew about it and had begun to replicate the miracle. Not only were statues of Lord Ganesha drinking milk, pretty much every God of the Indian pantheon had suddenly become thirsty.

The frenzy continued till late in the evening. By then, it had caused huge traffic jams in Delhi and other cities. Milk sales had spiked, and overall milk sale in Delhi was up 30%.

This milk miracle led to a lot of debate on gullibility of people. Scientists did experiments to try and convince believers that it was not a miracle but merely the effect of surface tension and capillary action.

What interests me in all this is not so much the miracle vs. science debate, but the speed and manner in which the news spread all over the world. Remember, this was in the year 1995. There was no Facebook or Twitter. No Internet. 24-hour news channels were not ubiquitous and mobile phones were at a nascent stage.

And yet the news spread. Fast!

~~~

April 18, 1775. The English still ruled America, though the war of Independence was on. A few people in Boston got to know that the English were planning a major offensive against the Americans the next day. There was no time to lose. At 10 pm that night, Paul Revere set out on his horse and rode North and then West of Boston. He informed people in the towns along the way that the British were coming and asked them to prepare for war.

At the same time, another rider, William Dawes, also left Boston and rode West with the identical message.

As it turned out, the towns that Paul went to, believed him and were well prepared for the British and were able to beat them back. On the other hand, William did not have much success in convincing the people he met that the news was genuine. As a result, those towns were not prepared and were surprised by the British attack.

Today, Paul Revere is revered as one of the greatest American heroes. The poet, Henry Longfellow, immortalised him in his poem, *Paul Revere's Ride*. If you go to Boston, you will find several references to him in the guidebooks. There are places named after him, his house is a tourist attraction, the US postal department issued a postage stamp to honour him and there is a statue of him in Boston.

Nobody remembers William Dawes.

~~~

Until the advent of Mahatma Gandhi, the freedom struggle in India was a very elitist movement. It is ironical that the Indian National Congress was itself the idea of an Englishman. Alan Octavian Hume, a British civil servant, thought it might be a good idea for educated and affluent Indians to form an organisation that could become the platform for civil and political dialogue with the Raj.

The first President of the Congress was a 'Westernised Oriental Gentleman' or WOG by the name of Womesh Chandra Bonnerjee. Note the spelling of the name; a clear indicator of his desire to be perceived as a loyal subject of the King. The original Congress had very limited ambitions and ended each of their meetings with a loyal singing of "God save the King".

The conditions for the emergence of Gandhi were set in the late 1800s with the rise of leaders like Bal Gangadhar Tilak, Bipin Chandra Pal and Lala Lajpat Rai. The three were together known as Lal-Bal-Pal and started the Swadeshi movement. These leaders were true nationalists who wanted more than the limited autonomy that was the demand of the moderates within the Congress.

However, the party was still in the hands of the elite Hindus and freedom was an abstract idea for most Indians. It really didn't matter to them who ruled in Delhi – their lives were unlikely to be affected by any changes.

Suman Srivastava

It took the genius of Mahatma Gandhi to understand that the only way India was going to gain independence was by involving the masses. In order to involve them, the idea of freedom had to be made more relevant and simple.

Out of this kind of thinking came the idea of the Salt Satyagraha. The idea was very simple. Let's not pay salt tax to the government.

~~~

Ideas travel. Sometimes fast, sometimes slow. Sometimes they die out quickly and without fanfare. Sometimes they spread through a whole community and form a movement.

How do ideas travel? What conditions do they need to spread far and wide? How can movements be triggered? How can these idea movements be used for marketing? These are questions that have been engaging the minds of several people and have led to a number of books. *Tipping Point* by Malcolm Gladwell, *Idea Virus* by Seth Godin and *Buzz* by Marian Salzman are the important ones that I have read.

The key conclusion that all these people draw is that not all human beings are created equal.

That's a pretty startling conclusion when you think about it. For centuries, human beings have lived in tiered societies. We have discriminated between people on the basis of accidents of birth. Some were born to be kings, others to be farmers. Some were born black, others were born Jews. Then over the past couple of hundred years, we got the idea that maybe all humans were created equal. This idea has led to democracy, capitalism and many other ideas of what we consider the modern society.

And now marketing gurus are telling us that human beings are not created equal.

Except this time the basis for segregation is based on their social values. Some people are always at the centre of their social networks and tend to influence their groups more than others. The opinions of these people seem to matter more than that of others who are usually on the periphery of their networks.

It turns out that people at the centre of the networks are critical in ensuring the spread of ideas. They can block ideas or help them spread. If they pass the ideas along, then they control the speed and direction of the ideas.

Buzz marketing has always been important. Word of mouth is, after all, the best way for a brand to advertise. Today, this has become more important than ever because of the power of social media. In order to do a good job in creating buzz, it is important to understand how and why some ideas create buzz and others don't.

Guru-speak: Tipping Point

It turns out that people at the centre of networks are critical in ensuring the spread of ideas. They can block ideas or help them spread. If they pass the ideas along, they control the speed and direction of the ideas.

Malcolm Gladwell talks about what it takes to reach a tipping point. A tipping point is one where the idea gets critical mass and moves from a small group into the general public. There is no stopping it after that point; the idea becomes an epidemic, spreading rapidly through society.

He identifies three rules - the law of the few; the stickiness factor; and, the power of context.

The law of the few refers to the few people who are critical in spreading an idea. They are not the idea creators, but the idea spreaders. These idea spreaders can be further divided into three groups - mavens, connectors and salesmen.

Mavens are people who collect information and use it as social currency. They collect information because they have a passion for that subject. It could be cars or technology or movies or food. Mavens will know everything there is to know about the subject. The best places to eat, what to order and when's the best time to go.

Mavens also love people. They genuinely want to help you. If they hear that you are looking for a place to eat, they will make sure they give you the best advice possible. Advice that is tailored to you and your tastes. Once you use that information and find it useful, your opinion of the maven will go up. And that's important to the maven.

A maven need not actually have been to the restaurants that he or she is recommending. So, it is not necessary for a maven to actually be a consumer of the product or service. Mavens just collect information and make sure that it is authentic. In fact, I think that one reason why mavens collect information is to get vicarious pleasure since they can't actually own the product. This is especially true for products like cars.

While mavens have a lot of information, they don't know a lot of people. Enter connectors who have a natural flair for knowing people. Connectors don't seem to believe that there are six degrees of separation between people. They seem to be able to find a link to virtually everybody in just one or two leaps. They get joy from knowing a lot of people and in constantly expanding their circle of acquaintances.

Connectors are the glue of communities. Groups tend to drift apart if the connector is, for some reason, not able to play an active role in that group. I'm sure you have had an experience of some group - your old school group for instance - that used to meet regularly until one of its connectors moved out of the city. Suddenly, the others don't seem to find the time to meet; unless, the connector is visiting.

The difference between mavens and connectors is one of emphasis. Mavens focus more on information while connectors focus more on people. Mavens may pass on the information to only five people, but each of those will buy into the idea. Connectors will ensure that the idea reaches ten people, though only five may believe it.

Malcolm Gladwell also identifies a third group of people. He calls them salesmen and their role is to spread the message. So mavens focus on the information, connectors on people while salesman on making people believe it.

These three groups make up the law of the few. These are the people needed to spread an idea. However, the idea needs some characteristics that allow it to spread.

Ideas need to be sticky and need fertile conditions to grow. Let's go back to the Indian freedom struggle. Gandhiji took the abstract idea of freedom and converted it into relevant and specific benefits for each group of people.

The farmers of North Bihar were suffering because they were forced to only grow indigo on their lands and then sell the produce to the British factories at very low prices. This had led to extreme poverty for these farmers. To these farmers, freedom meant the ability to choose which crops to grow on their land and to demand a fair price for it.

Similarly, the Salt Satyagraha appealed to a different group of people, while the boycott of foreign goods and the adoption of Indian made goods benefitted a third group.

In the language of Gladwell, Gandhiji made the idea of freedom sticky and used the power of context to help the message grow. Gandhiji made sure that the larger national movement was made up of various smaller movements. These local movements were closer to the lives of the common people and thus ensured greater identification and involvement. Of course, his ideas were spread by cadres of mavens, connectors and salesmen who were all members of the Indian National Congress.

Watch that Exponential Curve Go

Here is a little riddle. Imagine if I could take a sheet of paper and fold it fifty times. Yes, I know that it can't be done physically, but just imagine that it could be done. How high would this stack of paper be?

When I ask this question in a workshop, I get varied answers. Ranging from just an inch high to the height of the ceiling in the room. Even mathematically inclined people are able to say the formula (2^{50}) but aren't able to give me the result of that formula.

The correct answer is that the stack of paper would go all the way from the earth to the sun. Wow. That's really high and people always look at me incredulously. I know they are wondering if I am pulling their leg. But it's true. You can calculate it for yourself. Or see the calculations below.

Fold	Layers of paper	Fold	Layers of paper
0	1		
1	2	26	6,71,08,864
2	4	27	13,42,17,728
3	8	28	26,84,35,456
4	16	29	53,68,70,912
5	32	30	1,07,37,41,824
6	64	31	2,14,74,83,648
7	128	32	4,29,49,67,296
8	256	33	8,58,99,34,592
9	512	34	17,17,98,69,184
10	1,024	35	34,35,97,38,368
11	2,048	36	68,71,94,76,736
12	4,096	37	1,37,43,89,53,472
13	8,192	38	2,74,87,79,06,944
14	16,384	39	5,49,75,58,13,888
15	32,768	40	10,99,51,16,27,776
16	65,536	41	21,99,02,32,55,552
17	1,31,072	42	43,98,04,65,11,104
18	2,62,144	43	87,96,09,30,22,208
19	5,24,288	44	1,75,92,18,60,44,416
20	10,48,576	45	3,51,84,37,20,88,832
21	20,97,152	46	7,03,68,74,41,77,664
22	41,94,304	47	14,07,37,48,83,55,328
23	83,88,608	48	28,14,74,97,67,10,656
24	1,67,77,216	49	56,29,49,95,34,21,312
25	3,35,54,432	50	1,12,58,99,90,68,42,620

The distance to the sun is a mere 149.6 million km. So, even though the thickness of paper is very small, when it is multiplied by the large number (over one million trillion), the answer is huge.

How high would the stack of paper be if we fold it one more time? Did you start to multiply that large number by two? Or did you just say it is the distance from the earth to the sun and back?

The human insight that this exercise illustrates is that we cannot think exponentially. Human beings can think in arithmetic progression, but not in geometric progression. Even when it is explained to us, we do not really grasp the true significance of this.

The reason for bringing this up here is because this is how word of mouth works. You can start with a small number and that number can quickly grow very large.

Here is another illustration taken from Malcolm Gladwell's book, *The Tipping Point*. Suppose in a large town, fifty new people arrive who have some sort of a contagious disease. This disease is contagious only for a day, and on that day it tends to infect 2% of the people who meet the ill person. Now suppose that each of the affected people meet fifty other people in a day.

So fifty people meet fifty people of whom 2% get infected. This means that fifty people have infected fifty other people (2% of 2,500). If the newly infected people infect another fifty people, then this cycle can go on forever.

Now suppose an event happens. Perhaps, there is a festival resulting in increased human interactions. Thus, each of the fifty infected people meet 10% more people or fifty five new people. The 2% infection rate still holds. Now the exponential growth kicks in and within six months, over eighty million people will be infected.

This is the challenge for brands. We have to get a small number of brand advocates to start spreading the word. Even if they spread the word to only a small percentage of people that they meet, the word can spread very fast and soon you can have a really big hit on your hands.

The challenge is to get the right kind of advocates and get them truly dipped in your brand colour.

The Influence Spreaders

Indian advertising is celebrity crazy. All kinds of products from colas to cement, from cars to mobile phones, from suiting to underwear, use celebrities. What's worse is that many brands in the same category use celebrities in the same way and their ads end up looking quite similar.

The belief among marketers seems to be that film stars and cricket heroes are opinion leaders and will help create buzz for their brands. Well, there have been times when the celebrity has been used imaginatively and appropriately, and the strategy has worked for the brand. But often, the celebrity is remembered while the brand is forgotten. This is called the 'celebrity vampire' effect. In any case, the emphasis on opinion leaders is misplaced. Sociologists tell us that the key to creating buzz lies not in the opinion leaders, but in the opinion spreaders. And this is what we would talk about here.

The most common analogy for buzz is that of an illness causing virus. Each virus needs a carrier to help it spread. The malaria virus spreads through mosquitoes. The swine flu virus spread through pigs. Some viruses spread directly from one infected patient to another through air or through touch or through body fluids like blood.

If you were an evil villain and wanted to spread malaria in a certain area, what would you do? You would have to ensure there are a lot of infected mosquitoes in the area. You would ensure that conditions are right for them to reproduce and spread the virus.

Similarly, when we are good marketers and want to spread the idea of our brand, we will have to ensure that there are enough carriers of our message who go around spreading it. It is important to distinguish between the opinion leaders or the opinion creators and the opinion spreaders.

As mentioned before, Malcolm Gladwell believes that there are three types of people needed to spread an idea - mavens, salesmen and connectors.

Trends get started by innovators. But then there are people called mavens, who learn about these new ideas, understand them and get excited by them. They share these ideas with salesmen who find a way of communicating these ideas to the general public, and with connectors who are well respected in their communities and thus have high credibility. When the conditions are right, ideas spread through to the mainstream population. Or else, they flounder in the valley of death.

Marian Salzman, who was the Chief Strategy Officer in the advertising agency Euro RSCG (now called Havas), combined these three groups of people and called them Prosumers. The term is somewhat confusing as it has been used by different people in different ways. It was first used by Alvin Toffler in his book, *The Third Wave*, when he referred to people who were producers and consumers. Later, the term came to mean 'professional consumers' in categories such as audio hi-fi equipment. However, Marian Salzman uses the term to mean a proactive consumer - one who likes new things, seeks to find out more about them and then communicates these ideas to his or her circle of acquaintances.

I worked with Marian in the strategic planning function of Euro RSCG and we did a lot of empirical work to understand Prosumers and their effect on ideas. We found that Prosumers constitute 20% to 30% of every group. They are found in all social groups, regardless of age, education, income or any other demographic parameter. These are the people in a group who influence the group on which movies to watch, which places to eat out at, which mobile phone to buy and so on.

Prosumers help to bridge the gap between innovators and the mainstream. Hence, studying what the Prosumers think, gives marketers an early insight into how consumers (i.e. the rest of the market) would think later. At Euro RSCG, we found that it would take six to eighteen months for ideas to spread from Prosumers to consumers. So that was the lead that a smart marketer could have.

The Prosumers are the carriers of ideas. Understanding them, and then working with them, gives marketers a path to creating the elusive 'buzz' around their brands. In the next few chapters, we will study some cases where Prosumers have helped push an idea from the innovators into the mainstream.

Before we go, let's take a look at the social media ladder created by the consultancy firm, Forrester Research. This ladder shows that content on social media platforms are created by a very small number of people. A larger number comment on it and share it. The rest are happy just to view this content.

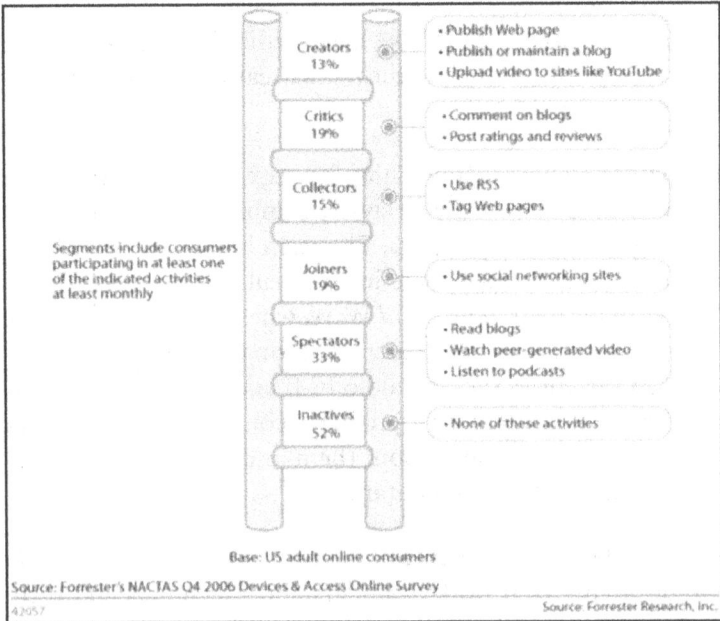

Creators 13%	• Publish Web page • Publish or maintain a blog • Upload video to sites like YouTube
Critics 19%	• Comment on blogs • Post ratings and reviews
Collectors 15%	• Use RSS • Tag Web pages
Joiners 19%	• Use social networking sites
Spectators 33%	• Read blogs • Watch peer-generated video • Listen to podcasts
Inactives 52%	• None of these activities

Segments include consumers participating in at least one of the indicated activities at least monthly

Base: US adult online consumers

Source: Forrester's NACTAS Q4 2006 Devices & Access Online Survey

Source: Forrester Research, Inc.

Social media strategies of brands too often focus on, and reward, the creators of the content. These strategies often ignore the people who are only interested in viewing content.

Once we understand the role of Prosumers, we may find that brands need to reverse this strategy. The focus has to be on having content online that is so compelling that people love to view it. We need to reward the viewers and the sharers, not so much the creators. In fact, the buzziest brands tend to be the creators of their own content (see the chapter titled 'The anomalous case of Apple', later in this section).

The Greatest Buzz Creator of All Time

Mohandas Karamchand Gandhi was the greatest buzz creator of all time. Long before the world had heard of the word 'buzz' or discovered the idea of the Prosumer, he had used these ideas to help India gain independence from the British.

Gandhiji understood that the idea of freedom was too remote for the masses of India to comprehend and get excited about. So he created an experiential campaign, actually several experiential campaigns. The 'Gandhi topi' and the 'Dandi Salt Satyagraha' were both well thought through and well executed experiential campaigns.

Before Gandhiji came on the scene, the Bal-Pal-Lal of Indian politics (Bal Gangadhar Tilak, Bipin Chandra Pal and Lala Lajpat Rai), along with a few other leaders, had launched the Swadeshi movement. The idea was to boycott all foreign made goods in the country and use only Swadeshi ones.

The idea was a good one. India was an important market for the British and a complete boycott would hurt them where it mattered - in their wallets. The movement galvanised many people from India's elite and middle classes and got them involved in the freedom struggle. Huge bonfires were lit in various cities where foreign goods were burnt. The movement gave a huge fillip to Indian businesses, and several Indian companies were established during that period. Companies like Calcutta Potteries, Bengal Chemicals and Bengal Lakshmi Cotton mills.

The Swadeshi movement involved the rich and the almost rich, but didn't really involve the poor who had no foreign goods to give up. That only happened after the arrival of Mahatma Gandhi.

Early on, Gandhiji tagged on to the idea of Swadeshi and suggested that everyone wore Khadi clothes, and, in particular, the Khadi cap. He wrote, "A Khadi cap, being clean and light, is wholly harmless. Moreover, to what better use could Khadi of the coarsest variety be put than making caps? One who is eager to dress himself in Khadi from head to foot should begin with the head straight away. The Khadi cap can be used by all, the rich and the poor... The conclusion should be that only the Khadi cap is to be regarded as Swadeshi. Such a cap needs no stamp. A Swadeshi cap should be one that could be identified even by children."

The Gandhi topi became the symbol of non-cooperation with the British. Let's quote Gandhiji on this subject again: "The wearing of white caps by Government servants has been officially regarded as a crime in the Central Provinces, and the decision has been publicly endorsed in the C.P. Council. The doctrine laid down by that Government is most servile and dangerous. If the white cap is the badge of the non-co-operation party, the use of Khadi may be equally regarded as such and penalised. And thus may Swadeshi become a sin in the Government dictionary. Foreign cloth was forced upon India two hundred years ago. The attempt has now commenced forcibly to prevent India from reverting to Swadeshi. Any well-meaning Government sensitive to public opinion would have encouraged the use of Khadi by its servants."

Gandhiji did not succeed in ensuring that the whole country wore the Gandhi topi. But he did succeed in creating a committed cadre of young people who became his ambassadors to the common man. For members of the Congress party, the cap became the symbol of the principles that they stood for and they wore it as uniform. The cap conferred a special recognition and status on the youth of the country and earned them respect from the rest of society. Gandhiji asked his followers who wore the cap to live up to the ideals it reflected. He wrote, "If, in spite of the Khadi cap that you wear, you have addictions, you will disgrace the cap."

Thus, Gandhiji used the cap to create his own band of Prosumers who spread his message across the country.

More modern 'movements' have all tried to have a wearable symbol. Anna Hazare's campaign against corruption used the Gandhi topi again, with the words 'I am Anna' inscribed on its side. The Livestrong campaign against cancer started by the now disgraced cyclist, Lance Armstrong, used a yellow plastic wrist band as its symbol. Other campaigns have used a variety of wrist bands, ribbons, badges and pins. The idea is that these symbols become a shorthand for the movement and create conversation opportunities where the Prosumers can propagate their mission.

Let's return to Gandhiji. Now that he had a cadre of committed followers, it was time for him to reach out even further to the real masses of India. This he did with the Dandi March against the salt tax.

Initially, people were surprised by Gandhi's choice of the salt tax. The Statesman, a prominent newspaper, wrote: "It is difficult not to laugh, and we imagine that will be the mood of most thinking Indians." The Viceroy, Lord Irwin, also did not take the threat of a salt protest seriously. He wrote back to London to report, "At present the prospect of a salt campaign does not keep me awake at night."

However, Gandhi was sure of his decision. The salt tax was a deeply symbolic choice, since salt was used by nearly everyone in India to replace the salt lost by sweating in India's tropical climate. An item of daily use could resonate more with all the classes of citizens than an abstract demand for greater political rights. The Salt tax represented 8.2% of the British Raj tax revenue, and hurt the poorest of Indians most significantly.

Gandhi felt that this protest would dramatise Purna Swaraj in a way that was meaningful to the poorest of Indians. He also reasoned that it would build unity between Hindus and Muslims by fighting a wrong that touched them equally.

After the protest gathered steam, the leaders realised the power of salt as a symbol. Nehru remarked about the unprecedented popular response, "It seemed as though a spring had been suddenly released."

Gandhiji started his March from Sabarmati Ashram in Ahmedabad on March 12, 1930. Over the next twenty four days, he walked 390 km to a small coastal village called, Dandi. Along the way, thousands of people joined the March. After he broke the tax laws on April 5, 1930, millions of Indians joined his movement. Nearly eighty thousand people went to jail along with him. The campaign continued for a year and was the first truly national and inclusive effort towards Indian independence.

So here is Gandhiji's tested formula for doing buzz marketing. As relevant today as it was in the year 1930:

- Have a simple, relevant message: Don't pay salt tax
- Create an experiential event around it: Dandi March
- Build a cadre of Prosumers to spread the message: Youth
- Provide them with a conversation starter: Gandhi cap

Lady Gaga and the Little Monsters

The reason this book is called *Marketing Unplugged* is that I believe that marketers can learn so much from musicians and the music industry. Musicians understand their fans better than marketers do.

Musicians have discriminated between their types of fans for a long time. A music app company called Bandsintown did a study that segmented music lovers on two axis - how engaged they were with their music and how social they were.

They found five distinct groups. A group they called Super Fans were people who were social, engaged with their music and had mainstream tastes. For them, going to a concert was really important since they loved being with people and loved their music. The Dedicated Diehards, on the other hand, would go to concerts primarily for the music. Music as a means to being social is not important to them.

The Soloists are people who love music but only in the privacy of their own homes. In contrast, the Tag Alongs aren't much into music, but like going to concerts because they value the social experience. The fifth group is of the Plugged Indies, similar to the Super Fans, but with a more independent taste in music.

Musicians like Lady Gaga and Justin Beiber have understood the importance of Super Fans and focus heavily on them. They seem to believe that the buzz created by these Super Fans will help fan their popularity with most of the other groups. Thus, Lady Gaga has her group of 'Little Monsters', while Justin Beiber has his club of 'Beliebers' who say they have the 'Beiber Fever'. Fan clubs such as these have their own salutations, ways of dressing and other ways of distinguishing themselves. Lady Gaga's Little Monsters have their unique 'Paws up' salute.

Lady Gaga is the ultimate social media super star. Lady Gaga was the first artist to reach one billion views on YouTube; she beat President Barack Obama to ten million Facebook fans (she now has around thirty five million fans on Facebook); and she was the first Twitter user to acquire 10 million followers.

So how has she done this? There are dozens of case studies, articles and blogs available online that try to glean out the key lessons that we can learn from her success. All of them talk, in some way, about being focused on her core fans and providing them content that makes them feel special. This content includes bonus tracks that only fans can get, photos of Lady Gaga, special offers and so on. Lady Gaga often talks about her 'little monsters' being the only people who matter to her. She even talks about her success as actually being the success of her fan club.

The question that arises is how she got started. This is where it is interesting to read about what her digital media agency, Think Tank Digital, has to say.

According to them, in the early days of her career, Lady Gaga made herself more available to bloggers than any other star before her. In the first six months, her agency managed to secure for her fifty interviews and ensured ten million impressions about her. In addition to making her available for interviews, the musician's record label released all kinds of assets that made great blogger fodder, from video clips to photos of her.

That sounds like a good old reach and frequency media strategy. She targeted reaching large number of people often enough to get noticed. Then she managed to create an impression –by being different and more authentic. And then the social media kicked in. Now all she has to do is to keep fanning the flames.

I think it is fair to say that she was successful because she was the first to implement this strategy. Copycats aren't likely to reach anywhere close to this level of success, even if their music is perceived to be better. That is the overall message of this book. Strategy needs to be different and unplugged to really succeed. Lady Gaga's strategy certainly was.

The Anomalous Case of Apple

Lady Gaga succeeded in generating buzz because she focused on social media. Apple seems to have succeeded in generating buzz by ignoring social media.

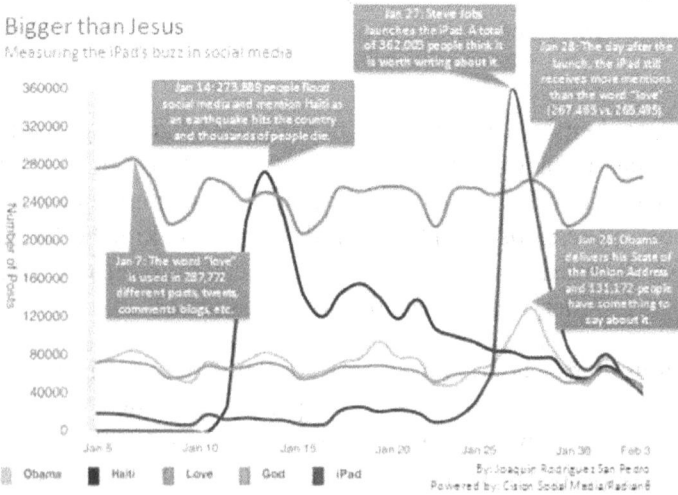

Apple has little direct presence in social media. No Facebook page, no Twitter handles, no You Tube channel for the main brand. Some of their product brands (App Store, iTunes, iBooks etc.) do have Facebook pages and Twitter handle, but even these don't respond to consumers. They simply send out marketing messages. They use social media like a mass media channel.

And yet there is more buzz on social media about Apple and its products than any other brand. Twitter seems to explode every time there is a new launch from the company. The chart above shows the buzz about the iPad and compares that with the buzz for Obama, Haiti (where there had been a big earthquake), Love and God. You can see the winner clearly.

This buzz isn't limited only to the USA. The map below shows the buzz created globally by the launch of iPhone 5s. This was hardly the launch of a revolutionary new product. In fact, it is the sixth generation of the phone. And yet, the buzz was enormous and global.

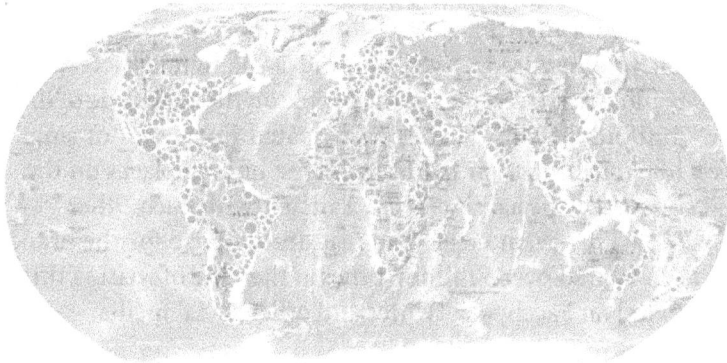

Apple, clearly, has got its act right. The question is what can the rest of us learn from this case.

Facebook, the brand, also breaks many of the tenets of social networking. Of course, it does have a Facebook page with millions of followers. But the posts are sporadic. Just a couple of posts a month. And even those are just announcements rather than conversations or discussions. Plus, they seem to ignore customer comments and feedback, at least publicly. But clearly, they have a lot of buzz too.

Coca Cola is another brand that is not very active on social media. Again, it does have a Facebook page with many million followers. But it is lackadaisical in posting to it. Again, no conversation at all. A friend, who works in a digital agency that has Coke as one of its clients, told me that the company is paranoid about any employee or agency saying anything controversial about them, so they would rather stay silent. They believe the risks of real time social media engagement are too high.

And yet, Coca Cola has buzz too. Lots of it. When we study the buzz around Coke, we may get a clue as to how these brands that ignore social media actually end up getting buzz.

In the year 2009, Coca Cola launched the 'Open Happiness' campaign. This started out as a regular advertising campaign - many commercials created with some great music. Coke found local musicians in each major market to create music around the theme of the campaign.

Then it went beyond the regular TV route. Coke created numerous events around the theme of 'open happiness'. The India - Pakistan peace initiative is an example. For this, the company set up a pair of connected vending machines, one in a mall in New Delhi and the other in Karachi. "Each vending machine featured a webcam and a giant touchscreen monitor. Passersby could grant free sodas to the people on the other side of the digital window - but only if both parties participated in a series of simple joint activities, like touching their hands to corresponding places on the screen, drawing concurrent peace signs, and dancing with each other." (Ad Age, May 20, 2013). This event created a great deal of buzz for the brand. This film has been viewed over 5 million times at the time of writing this. Plus it has been shared on Facebook, Twitter and other social media.

This holds a clue to getting buzz on social media. The secret does not lie in real time conversations with consumers. But in creating great content that people can talk about. A social media expert, Ramesh Srivats, said it very pithily. In an interview on CNBC's Storyboard show, he said: "The coolest brands today are built through actions, which people talk about... Brands do, people talk." He goes on to say that consumers don't go on social media to talk to their beer brand or share a joke with their bikes. So brands should not try to interrupt conversations that are going on and try to get involved. Rather, they should do things that get the consumers to talk about them.

Maybe, that is why Apple, Facebook and Coca Cola have a great deal of buzz even though they are not every active on social media. Their actions are talk worthy. Apple keeps creating great products and stages them in dramatic ways. Facebook keeps adding features to its site. And Coke creates events that bring a smile to our faces.

As Ramesh Srivats says, "Brands do, people talk." Of course, the action better be creative if you want buzz around it. Else you will sound pathetic.

Get People to Hate your Brand

Everyone wants to be loved. Nobody wants to be hated. Yet there is a thin line between love and hate. Scientists have found that the part of our brain that lights up when we feel love is the same part that lights up when we feel hate.

Brand managers would love to have everyone love their brand. They would love to turn every human being into an advocate. But human beings are different from each other. So brand managers try to live up to the cliché, 'all things to all people'. By doing so, they become bland and then find they have no advocates.

If you want some people to love you insanely, then it is almost essential to have some people who hate you insanely. Weak brands tend to be at the centre, while strong brands tend to take a definite stand.

This is most true of political brands. Think of the BJP. It is strong only when it polarises opinion. When it tries to become a reasonable party, people find it boring and drift away to the Congress camp. Thus, the Babri Masjid issue polarised people and led to the BJP coming to power at the centre. Then the party got less strident and lost power in the year 2004. The advent of Narendra Modi has made it extreme again. And so they won again.

Whether in power or not, the BJP has succeeded in becoming the reference point for political debate. Parties with ideologies similar to the BJP are now called 'Hindutva' parties, while the others define themselves as being 'secular'. There was a time when all the parties defined themselves with reference to the Congress. Today, the reference point has changed.

The strongest brands become reference points in their categories. Apple is not the volume market leader in mobile phones, but all competitors are trying to come out with 'iPhone killers'. There are lots of people who dislike the iPhone and have rude names for Apple fans. Perhaps, this opposition is what makes the fans into advocates.

This implies that brands should aim to be thought leaders rather than market leaders. Become thought leaders and market leadership will follow.

One of the better books on competitive marketing strategy is *Eat the Big Fish* by Adam Morgan. The point the author makes in the book is that there are more of challenger brands than there are leaders. Yet, most business and marketing books give examples of how leaders behave. Those lessons aren't relevant for challenger brands.

A challenger brand has to evolve an idea that is different from the perceived wisdom of the category. Then, it must put all its resources into evangelising that point of view and trying to own it. Challenger brands that are successful in doing so end up becoming leaders.

Before the iPhone, all phones had buttons. In fact, the trend was towards having full keyboards (Qwerty keyboards) on phones. Then iPhone came along and offered a phone with just one button. That was the signal that it was really different. You had to use your fingers in a simple and intuitive manner. That was the challenger idea of the iPhone - you needn't be a nerd to use a smartphone.

As discussed previously, before the Swatch watch came along, Swiss watches were made of precious metals, were expensive and had classical designs that lasted for generations. Swatch challenged those ideas and came out with cheaper plastic watches in many colours and designs. Now, you no longer had to have just one watch that you wore everyday. A watch could be your daily fashion accessory. In order to own this idea, Swatch spent its entire marketing budget on hanging a large watch down the side of a tall building in Zurich that said, 'Swatch. Swiss made. Sf15.'

This idea was sacrilege to many people. Swiss watches were known all over the world for their craftsmanship and were the ultimate in luxury brands that became heirlooms. Swatch got a lot of criticism, but also a lot of imitators. It was a polarising brand that became a global success.

Jack Trout, the marketing guru, has the same idea, but expresses it in a different way. He talks about 'repositioning' - the idea that you can get a position for yourself by creating a negative perception of your competitor. He urges you to "Never be afraid of conflict either. The crux of a repositioning program is undercutting an existing concept, product, or person. Conflict, even personal conflict, can build a reputation overnight." Ralph Nader got famous not by saying anything about Ralph Nader, but by going out and attacking the world's largest corporation single-handedly.

The best examples of repositioning come from politics. Here is Jack Trout again:

> "Karl Rove did enormous damage to John Kerry by repositioning him as a 'Flip Flopper'. This helped President George W. Bush set up his position of being a strong leader. Unfortunately, the Kerry campaign was too busy trying to position him as a Vietnam War hero instead of attacking the Bush record. They should have used repositioning against the Bush strategy by saying that President Bush was 'Strong but wrong.' "

Repositioning works only when used against a strong opposing brand, one that has a lot of people supporting it. Many of them will turn to hate you, thus getting recognition for the challenger.

In marketing we say, 'love me or hate me, but don't ignore me'

The Secret Growth Tonic of Bharat Matrimony

When Indians move to the United States, they seem to become more Indian than ever. They go to temples more often, celebrate more festivals and insist that their children learn about Indian culture.

Gay people seem to insist on letting everyone know that they are gay. At least once they are 'out of the closet'.

I am left-handed and feel a special kinship with everyone else who is a fellow southpaw.

There is something about humans that makes them want to identify with small groups. People don't want to belong to the faceless majority. When they are part of the majority, they find a way to divide the whole. Hence, the divisions on religious sects (Shia-Sunni, Protestant-Catholic etc), caste, sexual orientation, their dominant hand and so on.

One of the roles of a brand is to provide a sense of identity to its users. People believe that the brands they use say something about them. Whether it is their drink, their clothes, their mobiles or their cars, most people try to stay 'on message' with their brand choices. Thus, people who think of themselves as being rebellious actually have a pretty tight uniform of clothes they wear, the hairstyles they sport, the vices they have and so on. Remember the hippie look, the hippie lifestyle, even the hippie pose?

Prosumers, in particular, seem to have a high need to stand out of the crowd. They hate to use brands that everyone else uses, since that deprives them of any social currency. This behaviour is most apparent in musical tastes. Prosumers would discover a new band, talk about it to everyone and then, just when the band becomes popular, move on to another one. It's just not cool to listen to the most popular bands.

For brand managers, this can be quite disconcerting. They spend a lot of time and effort to make a brand cool. But as the brand climbs up on the popularity ladder, it climbs down on the coolness quotient. What is a brand to do?

Bharat Matrimony has an interesting solution to the problem. The brand is in the online matrimonial classifieds business. The perceived leader in the category is Shaadi.com and that is the brand name that people use to refer to the category. However, Bharat Matrimony is several times the size of Shaadi in terms of users as well as revenue. So how does it manage to not become a brand leader?

The answer is simple. It has sub brands that 'belong' to specific groups of customers. These sub brands are mostly on the basis of caste and religion. Currently, there are more than three hundred and twenty five different 'community matrimony' sites under the overall umbrella of Bharat Matrimony.

The range is truly astonishing. Not just Marwari Matrimony, but also Agarwal Matrimony. There are even sites called Elite Matrimony (for rich

The Largest Matrimony Group - Uniting Millions in Marriage

Over 325 exclusive community matrimony sites

Looking for a life partner from your community? Click on your community matrimony site below and get started

Popular Matrimony Sites

assamesematrimony · marathimatrimony · tamilmatrimony · muslimmatrimony

bengalimatrimony · marwadimatrimony · telugumatrimony · christianmatrimony

gujaratimatrimony · oriyamatrimony · urdumatrimony · sikhmatrimony

hindimatrimony · parsimatrimony · AssistedMatrimony · jainmatrimony

kannadamatrimony · punjabimatrimony · EliteMatrimony · buddhistmatrimony

keralamatrimony · sindhimatrimony

divorceematrimony

More Matrimony Sites   A B C D E F G H I J K L M N O P R S T U V Y

A	B	C	D
andhramatrimony	badagamatrimony	chambamatrimony	devadigamatrimony
adishaivamatrimony	baidyamatrimony	chandravanshkahar matrimony	ganiga matrimony
agarwalmatrimony	bakshamatrimony	chasamatrimony	deshasthamatrimony
agrimatrimony	baniyamatrimony	chhatradaivavanshyamatrimony	devadigamatrimony
ahommatrimony	balijamatrimony	chaudarymatrimony	devanga matrimony
ambalavasimatrimony	banikmatrimony	chaurasiamatrimony	devangamatrimony
ahavimatrimony	baniyamatrimony	chettiyarmatrimony	devangkoshti matrimony
aarkatnadmatrimony	banjaramatrimony	chhotrimatrimony	dhangarmatrimony
aruthathiyarmatrimony	balemmatrimony	chippolumatrimony	dheevaramatrimony
aroramatrimony	barendramatrimony	ezhavamatrimony	dhimarmatrimony
aryavaysyamatrimony	barimatrimony	coorgmatrimony	dhobamatrimony
audichyamatrimony	baruioilmatrimony		dhobimatrimony
avantikmatrimony	boistavmatrimony		dravidamatrimony
	chandalmatrimony		damamatrimony
	bhatamatrimony		duxadhmatrimony
	bhatrajumatrimony		
	bhatramatrimony		
	bhavasarkshatriyamatrimony		
	bhovimatrimony		
	bhusyhamatrimony		
	bilavamatrimony		
	boyermatrimony		
	brahminmatrimony		
	brahminmatrimony		
	bengalimatrimony		

More Matrimony Sites   A B C D E F G H I J K L M N O P R S T U V Y people) and Divorcee Matrimony. Something for everyone, and yet a special brand for each group to belong to.

How can your brand become popular and still remain a community that consumers can identify with?

ELEPHANT IN THE ROOM:

THE WORLD IS NOT FLAT

Globalisation Porn

Globalisation is a seductive idea. Life would be so much simpler if the whole world was homogenous.

The idea of globalisation is not new. Emperors always dreamt of ruling the whole world. Religious leaders seek to convert everyone. Businessmen have always looked to expand globally. From Alexander the Great to Adolf Hitler, from the early Christian missionaries to the contemporary Muslim Taliban, from the East India Company to Coca Cola.

All globalisers come up against the reality of differences between themselves and the people they want to conquer or convert. In the past, religious missionaries took it upon themselves to 'civilise' the savages.

Today, it is considered bad manners to want to change local culture. So marketers are doing the next best thing. They are hoping that the world will turn homogenous soon.

The website of the Global Policy Forum asks these questions:

"Technology has now created the possibility and even the likelihood of a global culture. The Internet, fax machines, satellites, and cable TV are sweeping away cultural boundaries. Global entertainment companies shape the perceptions and dreams of ordinary citizens, wherever they live. This spread of values, norms, and culture tends to promote Western ideals of capitalism. Will local cultures inevitably fall victim to this global "consumer" culture? Will English eradicate all other languages? Will consumer values overwhelm peoples' sense of community and social solidarity? Or, on the contrary, will a common culture lead the way to greater shared values and political unity?"

Well, a lot of marketers seem to hope that the answers to all the questions above would be 'Yes'. Even if they don't explicitly believe this, they implicitly do so, if they are to be judged by their actions. Marketers go to bars and nightclubs around the world and see people wearing jeans, drinking Bacardi and Coke and dancing to globally hit music. From this, they conclude that the youth in Shanghai, Mumbai, New York and London are basically the same, just at different points in the development cycle.

The biggest symbol of globalisation is Coca Cola. The brand is seen as a symbol of the American dream, freedom and of capitalism. People love and hate Coke for the same reason - that it is a symbol of a global culture. An excerpt from an article in BBC News Magazine: "It was the French who first coined the pejorative term 'coca-colonisation' in the 1950s. Trucks were overturned and bottles smashed, says Standage, as protesters saw the drink as a threat to French society."

Thomas Friedman has written a super-hit book, *The World is Flat*. The book concludes that the world is fast becoming truly global. It doesn't matter whether you are born in New York or Bengaluru, you now have the same opportunities to succeed.

Mr. Friedman identifies the ten forces that flattened the world. These include the fall of the Berlin Wall, which allowed us to think about the world as a single market, a single ecosystem, and a single community. It also includes the creation of the Netscape browser, which opened the Internet to everyone; the development of workflow software, which allowed individuals anywhere to collaborate on projects; and the scramble to fix the Y2K millennium 'bug', which caused the first big outsourcing of computer programming when companies needed softwares to be quickly rewritten. He also talks about networked production and integrated supply chains. Finally, he is enamoured by the rise of China and India.

So, essentially, Mr. Friedman thinks that technology is going to help create a global culture. This is a soothing conclusion that helps people make 'global' strategies in New York, London and Paris. The conclusion is so alluring that one writer (whose name I have forgotten) called it 'Globalisation porn'.

Unfortunately, not too many gurus agree with Mr. Friedman. This section will discuss the fallacy of the cliché that the world is flat.

They Just Look the Same

Marketing across cultures leads to some really funny situations. It is funny if it happens to someone else, of course.

A lot of boo-boos happen due to language problems. The translations are just terrible and not only do they not capture the meaning of the original, but actually end up saying something quite different.

China alone has a host of such stories to contribute to marketing folklore. Pepsi's slogan of "Come alive with Pepsi" was translated as "Pepsi brings your ancestors back from the dead." American Express' baseline "Don't leave home without it" became "Stay home with it". And Kentucky Fried Chicken found that it's tag line "Finger-lickin' good" had become "Tastes like human fingers".

This doesn't happen only in China, though.

An American ink manufacturer selling bottled ink in Mexico told customers that they could 'avoid embarrassment' (from leaks and stains) by using its brand of ink. The Spanish word used to convey the meaning of 'embarrassed' was 'embarazar', which means 'to become pregnant'. Many people thought the company was selling a contraceptive device.

A laundry detergent company found sales in Quebec slumping after introducing a new point-of-purchase campaign announcing that the detergent worked particularly well on the dirtiest parts of the wash - les parties de sale. The advertiser later learned that this phrase was similar to another Quebecois expression for 'private parts'.

An American airline in Brazil advertised the 'rendezvous lounges' in its jets, until they found that in the Brazilian brand of Portuguese, it meant a place to make love.

The problems aren't just with the language.There are other cultural cues that can be misunderstood.

A baby food company unsuccessfully tried to market its product with a label showing a cuddly infant in an African nation. It turned out that many of the prospective customers in Africa thought the jars contained ground-up babies.

A few years ago, a famous American designer began to advertise her new fragrance for women in the Latin American market. The advertising campaign emphasised on the perfume's fresh camellia scent. The fragrance did not move from the shelves of stores in Latin America at all because camellias are the flowers used for funerals in most of Latin America.

A detergent brand in the Middle East illustrated the power of its product visually by showing three frames. The first had a dirty garment, the second showed the garment dipped in a bucket of detergent solution and the third showed the sparkling clean garment. This was thought to be simple and fool proof. Except the team positioned the boxes from left to right, while Arabs usually read from right to left. So consumers were receiving the message that clean garments come out dirty after using the detergent.

I guess any group of international marketers can sit around swapping such stories. The point I'm making is not that people involved in the above cases were stupid. The point is to highlight the importance of culture in our marketing efforts.

A culture expert once told me that the most complex culture in the world is your own. All of us have been guilty of typecasting whole nations with a word or a phrase. I wouldn't be surprised if a Brazilian thinks that all Indians are techno geeks who speak English with a funny accent and eat vegetarian food. As an Indian, I know that isn't true and I know the difference not just between North Indians and South Indians, but between people from two neighbouring states and even regions within the same state. Hey, I can even tell who lives in South Bombay and North Bombay and differentiate between residents of East and West Bandra.

Of course, I think all Brazilians are fair, have awesome bodies, dance beautifully and are crazy about football. Hence, I cannot bank with Bradesco or Itau Banks, which are two of Brazil's most valuable brands.

Because I just can't associate conservative banking values with my image of Brazilians.

Guru-speak: World 3.0

Pankaj Ghemawat was admitted into Harvard University to study Applied Mathematics at the age of sixteen. At the age of nineteen, he was accepted to Harvard Business School's Ph.D. program in Business Economics. Later, he became the youngest full Professor at Harvard Business School and taught there for twenty five years. Ghemawat was also the youngest 'guru' included in the guide to the greatest management thinkers of all time published in the year 2008 by *The Economist*. You could say that he's quite a bright guy.

Dr Ghemawat wrote an article *The World isn't Flat* and followed it up with a book, *World 3.0*. These two pieces of work set him firmly in the opposite lobby to Mr. Thomas Friedman. Dr Ghemawat says that the whole point of his work is that there is too little data in the globalisation debate. As a result, people are forming opinions without a basis.

Interestingly, both supporters of globalisation and critics of it believe that globalisation is a reality. When asked what percentage of trade is global, most people guess a high number. Dr. Ghemawat provides some data.

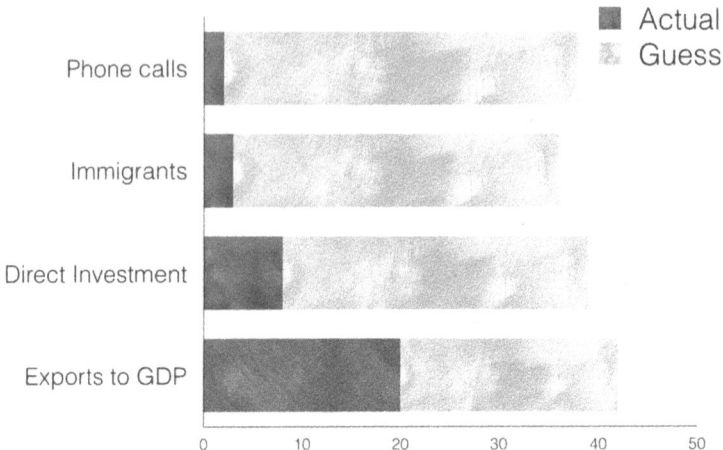

The lighter bars in the graph represent the average of the guesses that people make when asked what proportion of that factor is across national boundaries. The darker bars represent the actual facts.

So we see that only 2% of phone calls are across boundaries, only 3% of people in the world are first generation immigrants, only 10% of direct investments are from foreign sources and exports (in terms of value added) are only 20% of GDP. In all cases, the guesses are 30-40%.

People ask Dr. Ghemawat about Facebook. Since Facebook makes it easy for people to make friends across the world, it is interesting to see whether they actually end up making friends overseas. His research shows that most people's Facebook friends are actually from their own country and less than 20% of their friends are from abroad.

He then goes on to formulate his thesis about the four stages of globalisation. He numbers these four stages from World 0.0 to World 3.0.

World 0.0

At the earliest stages of civilisation, man lived in small clans where everyone was related by blood or marriage. In 3000 BC, experts estimate that there were nearly a million independent political entities. These separate 'countries' did not trade or interact with each other even though there were no regulations that prevented them from doing so.

World 1.0

This was the boom time. Dr. Ghemawat writes:

"Between 3000 BC and AD 2000, world population increased more than a hundredfold and gross world product more than a thousandfold in real terms. But by far the biggest change took place in the realm of social organisation: the world consolidated into fewer than two hundred independent political entities, implying a several hundred thousandfold increase in their average size, measured in terms of number of people."

Basically, mankind moved from living in clans to living in countries. These new countries had military might to protect their citizens from that of others. Most countries were self-contained culturally, socially and economically. Thus, there was very little integration with the rest of the world and there were strong regulations that prevented this.

World 2.0

Globalisation can be said to have started in the mid nineteenth century when the British and the Dutch formed their respective East India companies and sailed forth to trade with the world. These were the first multinationals, though the real growth of MNCs came in the last few decades of the twentieth century. Under Ronald Reagan and Margaret Thatcher, the era of lean government was upon us, with the idea that market competition was the best way forward. It was believed that national boundaries caused inefficiencies in trade and the focus should be on true globalisation.

People who believe that the 'world is flat', believe so because of technology. We have reached a state of a borderless world where goods, services, people and ideas can move freely across the globe. The data, of course, suggests that this is not so.

World 3.0

Dr. Ghemawat uses the diagram above to explain the various stages of globalisation. In World 0.0, there was no market integration or regulation. In World 1.0, there was a lot of regulation that resulted in countries being isolated from each other. Hence, there was little market integration. In World 2.0, people believe that there is complete market integration because all barriers to it have been brought down. Contrary to this belief, the reality is that we live in a world where there is a small amount of market integration and there is a fair amount of market regulation.

The dangerous bit of believing that we live in World 2.0 is that the benefits of it are being under-achieved and the fear of it is over-stated. Since we believe that the world is already globalised, the efforts to globalise may further reduce and thus, we would not benefit from the efficiencies of globalisation.

On the other hand, people who fear globalisation are in a state of panic because they see Coke and McDonalds everywhere, so their opposition is intensified. If they are assured that global transactions are a small part of the total, they may be more willing to do a sensible cost-benefit analysis of globalisation.

In his book, Prof. Ghemawat talks about the problems of doing business across the Canada - USA border. The two countries have a so-called open border and companies can freely trade in either country. However, in reality, there are several issues that prevent this from happening. Here is the case of Ganong Brothers, a candy maker from Canada (quoted from the book, World 3.0):

> "A company that fits the bill is Ganong Brothers, Canada's oldest candy maker and a firm roughly one-thousandth Google's size. While chocolates comprise its principal product line, what has really attracted attention is the company's attempt to sell jelly beans in the United States. Because of free trade agreements, there are no tariffs on jelly beans, and one might expect them to flow freely across the U.S.-Canadian border. And Ganong would seem well-positioned, literally, to serve the U.S. market: the state of Maine is just 1.8 kilometres away (1.1 miles for Americans) and visible from the offices of company president David Ganong. But it's not so simple.

> Take labelling as an example. In Canada, nutritional labels read '5 mg' with a space between the number and the unit of measure. Yet, Ganong's jellybeans can't get into America unless the nutritional label reads '5mg' without the space. Likewise, the two countries calculate daily nutritional values differently. The packages of jellybeans for American consumers need to state what percentage of an American's daily allotment of nutrients the product provides, even if this percentage varies only slightly from the daily allotment for a Canadian (e.g., 4% of the daily allotment of iron as opposed to 2%).

Such bureaucratic differences may seem trivial, but their effects are not. To comply with U.S. labelling laws, Ganong has to produce jellybeans in separate runs for its American and Canadian markets; this means that production runs for each batch are smaller and less economical. Separate bags for the two countries elevate the costs of packaging, and the company needs to spend more money and devote more warehouse space to store separate inventories of bagged jellybeans for the United States and Canada.

Lest it seem that the United States is unilaterally unreasonable, it's worth adding that Canada ties up trade in red tape as well. According to the Canada Border Services Agency, commercial importers into the country must register their businesses by obtaining a fifteen-digit business number. They must also create an accounting package for their shipments consisting of two copies of a cargo control document, two copies of an invoice, two copies of a Form B3 (Canada Customs Coding Form), any other required permits or forms such as health certificates, and in many cases, a Certificate of Origin form. Once shipments are reported to the government, they are granted a unique fourteen-digit transaction number before they are released by customs and any duties or taxes are paid. To handle all this red tape, American exporters usually hire an export agent, who contracts with a shipper or carrier, who in turn deals with a clearing and forwarding agent in the destination country, who in turn deals with the buyer. Bank letters of credit are often required, as is insurance on the part of the exporter. Of course, none of this counts the documentation that is required on the American side to export goods.

Since September 11, 2001, the barriers to trade have increased further due to the application of new layers of security and more complex rules and regulations. Processing time to enter the United States from Canada by truck (the principal mode of transportation) now takes three times longer than before. Delays have become such a problem that the Canadian government has employed a website devoted to tracking delays in real time.

These changes have directly affected Ganong Brothers. David Ganong related that his firm had a candy shipment delayed for five weeks so that the American government could analyse whether the yellow food colouring used in the product had been FDA approved. For four weeks, the government didn't reveal why the shipment was being held, what they were checking and what it would take to get it released. With Ganong's American customers expecting just-in-time delivery, surprise hold-ups such as these leave them looking elsewhere for more reliable sources."

So we don't live in a flat world after all. National boundaries do matter. But more than national boundaries, what matters for marketing are cultural boundaries. Let's move now to look at culture. How to measure it and how to deal with it?

The Man Who Measured Culture

The Netherlands is a small country in Western Europe, with a population that is less than that of Mumbai. Large parts of the country are below the sea level and prone to flooding. This country should have been quite irrelevant in the global scheme of things. Yet, it is a major economic power. What is the reason for this anomaly? Experts attribute the success of the Dutch to their global outlook. From the sixteenth century onwards, the Dutch have been venturing into the sea to find new lands to trade with. The Portuguese found the sea route to India, but it was the Dutch who set up the first independent base in the East.

It is, thus, appropriate that the world's leading expert on global cultures is a Dutch. Gert Hofstede was a psychologist who joined the Human Resources department of IBM in the year 1965. From the year 1967 to the year 1973, Hofstede administered cultural questionnaires to IBM employees in thirty countries. Later, he expanded his study to forty countries and regions. This chapter summarises the results of his study.

Dr Hofstede found that there were five dimensions on which the cultures of different countries could be measured. He had initially come up with four dimensions, but added the fifth one after studying China. Here are Hofstede's five dimensions:

Power Distance

This dimension measures the degree of equality in society - the higher the score, the more the inequality in the culture. In the graph below, we can see

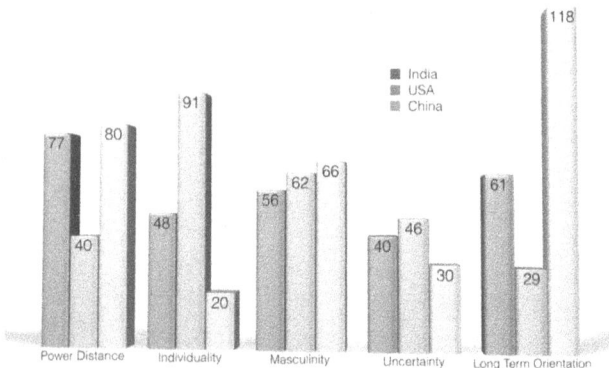

India
USA
China

Power Distance · 77 · 40 · 80
Individuality · 48 · 91 · 20
Masculinity · 56 · 62 · 66
Uncertainty · 40 · 46 · 30
Long Term Orientation · 61 · 29 · 118

that India and China have high power distance scores. Both are hierarchical societies and the cultural values differ from one class of society to another. In India, we have had the caste system for nearly five thousand years and it is ingrained in us that some castes are higher than others.

Individuality

Individualistic societies are loosely knit and individuals are expected to take care of themselves and their immediate families only. In contrast, a collectivist society is tightly knit with emphasis being on the clan, the extended family or the tribe rather than just the individual. In the former case, the emphasis is on 'I', while in the latter, it is on 'We'.

Anglo Saxon countries like the USA and Australia are very high on individuality, while countries like China are on the other end of the spectrum. India is in the middle with strong focus on the family and the 'kul' (clan), and this sets boundaries to what is allowed. However, within that circumference, the individuals have a fair amount of leeway to do their own thing. This is like a long rope that is tied to a post. The individual can wander wherever he or she likes, so long as the rope is not cut. Today, this rope has become longer than ever, but it is still very much there.

Masculinity

Masculinity is about achievement, heroism, assertiveness and material reward for success. Society, at large, is more competitive. Femininity is about cooperation, modesty, quality of life and caring for the weak. A feminine society is more consensus-oriented.

Scandinavian countries like Sweden are low on this dimension, which means that modesty is more highly prized than bravado. Japan is at the other extreme and it is all about heroism. Remember the Kamikaze pilots? They were revered in Japan as brave soldiers who voluntarily went on suicide missions in defence of their country.

Uncertainty

The uncertainty avoidance dimension expresses the degree to which the members of a society feel uncomfortable with uncertainty and ambiguity. So countries that are high on this dimension have rigid codes of conduct and are quite intolerant of deviations from it. At the opposite end are countries that are more relaxed about the future and focus more on practices than principles.

Japan is high up on this dimension. It is a very formal society with defined ways of doing everything. There is even a ceremony for having tea. Anglo Saxon countries are quite low on this dimension, but what is interesting is that India and China are similar to them.

Long Term Orientation

This was the dimension that Dr. Hofestede brought in after studying the culture in China. Here is how 'The Hofstede Centre' defines this trait:

> "The long-term orientation dimension can be interpreted as dealing with society's search for virtue. Societies with a short-term orientation generally have a strong concern with establishing the absolute Truth. They are normative in their thinking. They exhibit great respect for traditions, a relatively small propensity to save for the future, and a focus on achieving quick results. In societies with a long-term orientation, people believe that truth depends very much on situation, context and time. They show an ability to adapt traditions to changed conditions, a strong propensity to save and invest, thriftiness, and perseverance in achieving results."

Given that this dimension was invented especially because of China, it is not a surprise that China scores high on it. Anglo Saxon countries are nearly at the other end of the spectrum and India is in the middle. Japan is pretty high up on this too. Their companies did well in the last few decades of the twentieth century by taking a long term view, while their western competitors were more focused on the short term.

Hofstede's work is important because it is the first major global study which compares cultures across quantitative parameters. The data he used may be old, and, in any case, may not really represent the whole country since his sample was made up only of IBM employees. However, it does give us a theoretical framework to truly understand and analyse culture. We turn now to another guru who shows us qualitatively how different cultures perceive the same product.

Guru-speak: Culture Code

Culture is important for marketing. For international marketing AND for domestic marketing. Culture is the filter through which consumers receive marketing messages; if you don't understand the filter, then you will not know how your marketing message is being received. The distortions will lead to results that are completely different from what you desire.

Clotaire Rapaille, the author of *Culture Code*, says that we have always known about two kinds of layers beneath the conscious one in our brains. Freud found one layer that is the individual unconscious, while Jung found the other which is the collective unconscious. Now Rapaille proposes a third layer, the cultural layer.

The individual unconscious is due to the stored experiences of every individual. We may have 'forgotten' something that happened to us as a child, but it stays with us in our subconscious and influences us in ways that we are unable to explain. Similarly, the collective unconscious is something that is common to all human beings. Perhaps, we can call this instinct.

Between these two layers is a layer that has been inserted due to the culture that we live in. Maybe all human beings are a little afraid of the dark, since we are programmed that way. That is an example of collective unconscious. Some of us may associate night time with happiness because that is the time the whole family got together when we were children, so we have happy associations with the dark. That is individual unconscious. We may think of the colour black as being sophisticated or as being unlucky. That depends on our cultural unconscious.

Dr. Rapaille believes that we spend too much time trying to understand consumer's conscious mind and we don't even begin to understand what is really important - the cultural code. His book gives examples of codes from different categories for American consumers and helps to start thinking of whether or not our message is "on code".

He lists out five key principles.

Principle 1: You can't believe what people say.

Principle 2: Emotion is the energy required to learn anything.

Principle 3: The structure, not the content, is the message.

Principle 4: There is a window in time for imprinting the meaning of the imprint. This varies from one culture to another. For example, French taste alcohol as kids, while Americans only as teenagers.

Principle 5: To access the meaning of an imprint within a particular culture, you must learn the code for that imprint.

These principles will become clearer as we go through examples, but before we start, let's look at the process that Dr. Rapaille employs to understand cultural codes. He does three hour long sessions with consumers. In the first hour, he asks consumers to imagine that he has come from outer space and knows nothing about the product they are discussing. He asks them to describe the product and the stories around it. In the second hour, he gets consumers to make collages of words to describe the product. In the third hour, he switches off the lights and makes consumers lie down comfortably on the floor. He then talks to them (softly, I imagine) about their earliest memories associated with the product.

Sounds like a normal focus group, except for the last hour. But through this technique, he is able to reach down to a level that ordinary research is not able to. The answers he gets sound startlingly different and yet obviously true.

This is not the only way to understand culture. Watching movies may be a good way too! Certainly, cinema is a good reflection of a society and its culture, as are its popular TV shows, music and other art forms.

Semiotics is the science of signs. It studies cultural symbols and subsequent changes in these symbols to understand trends and predict them. Using semiotics and applying its techniques is a good way to understand cultural codes.

Let's start to understand cultural codes by looking at the code for alcohol in America versus the code for it in France. In France, children could start getting a sip of wine or champagne when they are still quite young. Kids grow up associating alcohol with celebrations.

In the USA and several other cultures, alcohol is forbidden and the first experience of it that a person gets is in the late teenage years. Often, that experience is negative in some way. Most of the words in English that are associated with alcohol are negative. You have shots and you get smashed. Sometimes, you get dead drunk. You try to drink the other person under the table, and generally get wasted.

Dr. Rapaille suggests that the American code for alcohol is a Gun. You can pull the trigger and that leads to consequences like getting dead drunk, smashed and wasted.

This is true for Anglo-Saxon and some other cultures, but not true for the French. It is also not true for a few other cultures that have not yet been globalised and retain their ancient codes.

Another interesting example is that of the Jeep. In America, the code for Jeep is a horse. Americans dream of the Wild West, of going to new places off the beaten path. The Jeep allows them to do that. They may not actually drive cross-country, but the image that they have is that of a horse.

In contrast, most of Europe associates the Jeep with liberators. The troops that came into Paris and other occupied areas to liberate them from the Nazis, came in Jeeps. Hence, the unconscious association of the Jeep is with liberation.

In India, we have grown up with the notion that the Jeep is driven by men who wield authority. The police, the army and other government officials drive the Jeep. So we associate the Jeep with power.

One would think that emotions are basic to human beings and should be seen in the same way in all cultures. But this turns out to be untrue. Take Love for instance. According to Dr. Rapaille, it has completely different codes in the USA, France, Italy and Japan.

In America, love is held to a very high standard. People there expect so much from love that they are often disappointed. Hence, the code for Love in America is False Expectations.

In France, love is almost a synonym for passion and pleasure. So the idea of love and pleasure is intertwined. Partners must focus on getting pleasure and giving pleasure to their partners. That is true love.

Italians, however, think love is something to laugh at. They regard it as a kind of comedy. They must have fun or else they find love to be unfulfilling.

The Japanese are completely different from all these cultures. They think of love as a temporary disease that afflicts the young. They seem to believe that the young are too young to know what love is.

Dr. Rapaille explains these differences by talking about the age of different cultures. America is a young culture that is barely in its adolescent phase. Japan is at the other end of the spectrum and is a very old culture.

The fact that America is culturally adolescent means that it can produce world beating products for the young. Levis jeans, Coca Cola, violent movies, youthful music (rock, hip hop, pop) are youthful products that America leads in. In contrast, it is yet to produce a truly great classical composer.

Americans love youth so much that they adore adolescent behaviour even in their icons. Look at the number of eccentric sports persons that the USA has produced - Andre Agassi, Williams sisters, John McEnroe, Mohammed Ali. Their bad behaviour has made them even more popular than just their performance would have.

Americans even want their leaders to be youthful, and often eccentric. Obama beat McCain to become President. Bill Clinton, George Bush and Jimmy Carter have all had very youthful personalities. The last 'old' president was Ronald Reagan, and he came through as being really young in his ideas and attitudes.

In contrast, the English think of youth as being slightly boring. Culturally, they like maturity and expect their leaders to act in a reserved manner even when they are young. In India, we think of youth as a stage in our lives, not the destination. So while Americans try to hang on to their youth for as long as they can, Indians want to move on to the next stage where they get more respect and adulation. Even in today's more westernised culture, seniority gets a lot of respect in India.

The contrast between the American and Indian cultures comes through in other areas as well. Take work. Work is really important for an American and tends to define his identity. Of course, there are writers and poets in America campaigning against that idea. In fact, Americans of all ages seem to be constantly going off on journeys to find themselves. However, these examples actually prove that the dominant belief in American culture is that work defines who a person is.

In India, it is the family that defines who you are. For five thousand years, we have lived with the notion that the individual is not as important as the family, the sect, the caste or the community as a whole. We measure the importance and status of people in terms of their background. It's so deep in our cultural psyche that our modern selves have not succeeded in completely eradicating it. We will discuss this in greater detail in the next chapter.

Once you start looking for the cultural codes, you can see them everywhere. Take food, for instance. Americans regard food as fuel. Something that they need to quickly put into their body so that they can go ahead and do the work that defines them. They end a meal with the statement, "I am full." Hence, they emphasise quantity and speed with respect to their food. It is not an accident that American restaurants give you such large potions of food. Nor is it a surprise that the Americans introduced the concept of fast food.

The French end their meal by saying, "That was delicious." Look at the emphasis of quality over quantity. They truly appreciate delicate tastes and take their time to savour food. Even children in kindergartens are taught to sit down at a table and eat their lunch slowly and carefully. The French actually look at fast food in a bewildered manner. They can't understand why food should be fast.

Indians are bewildered by self-service with respect to food. In our culture, we have never learnt to serve ourselves. Food is always served on our plates by others. By our mothers at home, the kar sevaks in a gurudwara or the hosts at a wedding. Therefore, when we are now asked to serve ourselves in a buffet, we tend to heap our plates with more food than we need. It all looks terribly uncultured. Of course, it is against our culture.

We can go on and on discovering the deep cultural codes for everything that we use in our daily lives. We can find cultural codes for ourselves and for foreigners who we deal with. The French think of Americans almost as an alien race. Dr. Rapaille calls the code, 'space travellers'. The Germans think of Americans as being cowboys. They consider them to be primitive people who are not as cultured or sophisticated, but at the same time as liberators and benevolent people. Hence, John Wayne.

The English think of Americans as being loud, crass, vulgar and big, but admire their confidence, passion and success. So their code for America is 'unashamedly abundant'.

Everyone has codes for their own country too. According to Dr. Rapaille, the French code for France is Idea. The English code for themselves is Class, while the German code is Order. One can instantly see why this is so.

What is the Indian code for ourselves? Think about it. We will get an expert's view of this next.

Guru-speak: Being Indian

India is one of the two rising countries of the century so far. The whole world is interested in understanding the country and its people. It is no surprise, therefore, that there are dozens of good books written on India by Indians living in India, non resident Indians, foreigners visiting India and by foreigners who have settled down in India. Each author brings in a unique perspective on our complex country.

I have three shelves in my bookcase filled with books on India. From this embarrassment of riches, I have chosen to base this chapter on a book written by Pavan Varma called *Being Indian*.

This book is an eye opener for Indians too. It analyses myths that we have about our culture and ourselves, and shows us the truth about ourselves. It is, moreover, extremely readable.

India is a very large and diverse country. Anything that you say about India, the opposite also equally holds true. However, myths get built using selective data points. These data points become part of a story that we build and start to believe in. The reality may be a bit more complex than the myth.

India won its independence with a non-violent struggle. And we have never invaded another country. Surely, this proves that we are non-violent people?

Similarly, we can point to the fact that we have been a democracy since the year 1947 and have the largest number of voters eligible to exercise their franchise. That couldn't have happened if we didn't have a democratic temperament.

India is the home of many religions. We have lived together for centuries and some of our religions focus on the afterlife. Surely, these facts mean that we are spiritual in our outlook, we are not materialistic and we are very tolerant.

Finally, we are not a homogenous country. We have so many diverse cultures that co-exist peacefully. This could be taken as evidence that we are eclectic and accept inputs from diverse sources.

So Indians are non-violent, democratic, spiritual, tolerant, un-materialistic and eclectic people. This belief is held by Indians and foreigners alike. Mr. Varma suggests that the educated Indian is to be blamed for creating this misguided belief. However, I believe that he is being too harsh. Perhaps, this is the narrative created by British social scientists, who first got fascinated by India during the British raj.

Either way, the myths are here to stay.

The history of India is a story of groups of people trying to improve their 'auqaat' or status in society. This is one of the fundamental truths that help us understand the Indian culture.

Indian society has been organised by the rules of the caste system for over five thousand years. It all started as a way of describing the professions. Thus, the priests were called Brahmins, the rulers and warriors were the Kshatriyas, the farmers and traders were Vaishyas and the workers were Sudras. Other groups such as tribals, nomads and foreigners were excluded from the caste system and were considered untouchables - now called Dalits.

It is believed that the Brahmins emerged from the head of God, while the Kshatriyas were born from the arms. God's torso gave birth to the Vaishyas and his legs to the Sudras. This belief led to a hierarchy that had Brahmins at the top and the Sudras at the bottom. This pecking order continues to this day. Your 'auqaat' was determined by where you are placed on this societal ladder.

Individuals were born into a particular caste and that's where they stayed for their entire lives. As individuals, they were not able to move up or down the hierarchy. However, sub-castes or 'jatis' were able to do so. Working together as a group, a 'jati' could move up the ladder by changing their profession or their rituals or by just moving into a new location.

So while the caste system is normally thought of as an inflexible structure, it actually allowed for a lot of movement within it. There was a constant struggle among the 'jatis' to improve their 'auqaat' and to prevent themselves from being pushed down the ladder.

The caste system may have become weaker over time, but not our belief in 'auqaat'. When two Indians meet each other for the first time, they try to figure out who has the higher 'auqaat'. This may be judged not just by their caste but also their designation, age or some other attribute. Once established, the person with the lower 'auqaat' will always show respect to the other.

This respect is shown in many ways. In the manner of addressing someone (aap and tum in Hindi), in the body language, in not being seated when the person with more 'auqaat' is standing. Also, in laughing hysterically at the most inane jokes cracked by a senior person.

To see this in action, observe people working in the government. Civil servants at all levels exude power, but only so long as their senior is not present. The change from alpha male to servile sycophant is dramatic and instantaneous when a senior enters the room.

A related concept to 'auqaat' is the behavioural trait of 'chamchagiri' or sycophancy. A person with lower 'auqaat' has to do 'chamchagiri' to the person with the higher 'auqaat'. This is also quite deeply ingrained in us.

Equality is not a value that is ingrained in our culture. We inherently believe that human beings are created unequal and we are willing to pay our respects to those above us on the ladder and look down on those below. Of course, if a senior person loses power, we instantly change our behaviour towards him. All our 'chamchagiri' is transferred to the new person who has acquired power.

Every decision gets taken in this unequal way. The senior person gets to decide everything from big decisions to trivial ones. Even groups of friends informally elect a leader and then follow him or her.

As Hofstede said, our power distance is high. He found the Power Distance Index for India to be seventy seven compared to a world average of fifty six. This is the highest score of all the dimensions for India and shows that it is the most dominant trait.

Once we understand the importance of 'auqaat' and the consequent hierarchy in Indian society, several other traits fall into place. It is natural that we are jealous of those above us and want to bring them down. Therefore, the people who are more successful need to guard against the negative vibes being sent out by those below. Hence, the concept of 'nazar utarna' - warding off the evil eye. There is a flourishing industry focused on selling products that ward off the evil eye. The more 'auqaat' you have, more the evil eye and more the need for products that deflect nazar.

If there is one thing that is more important than 'auqaat', it is 'izzat' (respect or esteem). We are willing to do anything to preserve our 'izzat' or prevent if from being lowered. Again, we hear of people killing close relatives including children, brothers and sisters in order to preserve the 'izzat' of the family. Mr. Varma asserts that often our responses to perceived deficiencies in 'izzat' can be totally disproportionate to the original slight.

Now that the caste system is less important in Indian society, one would have hoped that society would become more egalitarian. However, that has not proven to be the case. The current economic boom has created it's own set of winners and losers. People are now even more acutely conscious of where they stand in the new pecking order. 'Auqaat' still rules.

Almost any kind of product can be sold in India on the basis of 'auqaat'. Onida had a famous campaign that proclaimed: 'Neighbour's envy, owner's pride.' That was totally on code for India. Rin has used envy to sell detergents. Pan masala commercials routinely use status to sell their products. The list is endless.

According to Pavan Varma, our belief that we are not materialistic is belied by our scriptures. Think of the Mahabharata. The basic story is that of a property dispute between two sets of cousins that leads to an all out war between them. God, in the form of Krishna, actually advises Arjun to fight against his uncles, teachers and cousins rather than give up the property.

Even the Ramayana proclaims that it is better to be dead than to be poor. It goes on to exhort people to accumulate wealth.

Our Gods are materialistic too. Except for Shiva, all the other gods seem to love the good things in life. Human beings need to offer material goods to our gods in order to please them. No wonder that the richest trusts in India are the ones that run temples.

The thing is that Indians like everything to be cloaked with higher order philosophy. The Pandavas were said to be fighting for Dharma or righteousness rather than merely property.

A successful business community in India is of the 'banias'. Their credo is that 'dhanda' is their 'dharma'. Their business is their religion. This makes them very focused on their work and is probably a key factor in their success.

Apart from being materialistic, we are not really a very moralistic people either. Hinduism is probably the only religion in the world that does not have a concept of absolute evil. Nothing is banned. Everything is permitted under certain circumstances. It is OK to kill or lie or steal, provided you have to do it in the defence of Dharma. We know that Yudhishthir had to lie in the Mahabharata and have several other mythical stories where otherwise virtuous people had to commit a sin for a higher purpose. Hindus believe that the end justifies the means.

Notice again the importance of the higher purpose. We see this in the most popular TV serials and movies also. Good guys may commit adultery, but only because they had to. Bad guys commit adultery just for pleasure.

So we are status conscious, we are materialistic and we do everything we can to move up the 'auqaat' ladder. When you take these together, they add up to making us great entrepreneurs.

Introducing 'jugaad', the great Indian trait that enables us to come up with innovative solutions to any problem. We revere people who are 'jugaadus'. People who find a way out of the toughest situations. It could be a way to get a movie ticket when the board says 'house full' or it could be a way to make a tractor out of scrap material. We always manage some 'jugaad'.

It is not a surprise that Indians are great entrepreneurs. We have the motivation, the work ethic and the intelligence. In other words, 'dhanda' is our 'dharma', so we will do 'jugaad' to ensure that our 'auqaat' goes up.

Having said all this, the opposite is true as well. The ability to hold and reconcile two contradictory ideas at the same time is an important Indian trait. This is the characteristic that most baffles the western mind.

The great Indian mathematician Ramanujan used to say that 'Devi' would come to him in his sleep and write the proofs of mathematical theorems on his tongue. When he woke up, all he had to do was write it down on paper. This would exasperate his mentor, Hardy, who considered himself to be a 'fanatical atheist'. Hardy simply could not understand how a man of science could also have such blind faith in religion.

We see Indians create other strange combinations. Technology and religion combine to give us the online 'aarti'. We use online banking channels to give donations to temples. Men of science turn to astrology when it's time for their daughters to get married. We prefer arranged love marriages to both the other alternatives.

Dhanda is our 'dharma', so we should focus on excellence. However, we also have the 'chalta hai' attitude, which means we are happy to make compromises. A lot of observers attribute our under-achievement to this attitude. We can see this in our sports persons (especially those from an earlier era). Vijay Amritraj was an extremely talented tennis player. When he was a junior, experts used to talk about the ABC of tennis - Amritraj, Borg, Connors. While Borg and Connors went on to become legends of the game, Amritraj was never even able to break into the top ten players of the game. People say that he had the talent, but perhaps not the killer instinct. Was the 'chalta hai' attitude to be blamed?

Pavan Varma uses the analogy of furniture to explain the difference between the western and the Indian minds. The western mind is like an American closet. Everything in it is thrown together and interacts with everything else. The Indian is like a chest of drawers where the different selves co-exist in mutually exclusive zones. The foreigners can never predict which of our various selves will turn up in a given situation.

Another way to look at the difference between the western mind and the Indian one is to compare our music and our food. The western classical music has a linear structure with a clear beginning, middle and end. The Indian version is cyclical where a musician can explore the same raga in five minutes or five hours. Similarly, westerners eat their meals in courses where one taste does not interfere with the next. In India, we eat in a 'thali' where all the various courses are served at the same time. It is up to the individual to mix and match as he or she deems fit.

What can we do with all this information? Is it at all relevant for marketing?

Well, yes. Here are some tenets from Pavan Varma that could help us in understanding Indians and how to market for them.

Sukh sampatti ghar aaye: This is a big goal for Indians. We want prosperity and believe that happiness comes from it. So Indians are keen to receive our marketing messages and are far from getting conflicted by them.

The end justifies the means: We are result oriented rather than process oriented. We are willing to forgive anything so long as the end is good. Rich business tycoons have been forgiven for their unscrupulous behaviour en route their current level of eminence. I think that the organisers of the recently concluded Commonwealth Games in India will be forgiven on charges of corruption and incompetence because the Games were a success in the end. That is just the Indian nature.

Apni 'auqaat' mat bhool: Don't ever forget status. Indians are driven by it and you can't easily go against five thousand years of tradition. Your product probably has a status angle. Find it.

Izzat and ideology: Ladder your benefits until you reach a higher order. We love having everything wrapped in ideology. The 'Jaago Re' campaign of Tata Tea was so successful because of this insight.

Buri nazar wala tera muh kala: Since we like status so much, we also enjoy making others envious. Use the emotions of envy and one-upmanship to sell your products.

Jugaad: We like products that are all rounders rather than ones that are specialists. Our brands must appear to be partners in the entrepreneurial spirit of our customers. If a product has more than one use, Indians will find them all and love your brand as a result. Nirma detergent powder was used not just to wash clothes, but also to wash dishes, floors and bathrooms.

Melting pot of India: India is a blend of many cultures. We love this remixed culture and find the purist too stiff and uncomfortable. We prefer Hinglish to both perfect English and 'shudh' Hindi.

Chest of drawers: Indians are schizophrenic. Reach out to different aspects of their personality. How can you blend two opposite thoughts? Can you provide traditional goodness in a modern package?

Hota hai: Indians are optimistic people. Look at the poorest amongst us. Foreigners are constantly surprised by how positive and happy they sound even when they seem to have nothing to be happy about. So be positive. Fear never sells like happiness does. Look at the example of Saffola. For years it used the fear of heart attacks as the reason to buy it, but stayed as a niche brand. Then they started to use humour in their ads and the sales soared.

ELEPHANT IN THE ROOM:

BRAND IDENTITY IS NOT SACRED

Hello Brands, I can Read Now

The seals of Mohenjadaro were found in the remains of the oldest civilisation known to man, the Indus Valley Civilisation. Archeologists speculate that these might have been used to tag goods to indicate which craftsman or merchant had made them. An early example of branding, perhaps.

The practice of branding cattle as a means of ownership dates back to the ancient Egyptians. The practice continues to this day in parts of the world. In the USA, cowboys branded their cattle so that livestock from different ranches could graze together on open fields and the owners could still tell them apart. These brands were fairly crude symbols that were affixed on the hides of the cattle using hot iron.

For a long time, brand symbols had to be visual and, often, quite crude. Brands had to account for the lack of literacy among the general population and also for the poor reproduction techniques. Reproduction techniques have improved, but literacy is still an issue for brands catering to the masses. Even today, illiterate consumers recognise brands through the colour and graphics on the pack rather than the brand name. They even refer to the product by the product's symbol e.g. 'kachua chaap'(tortoise brand).

Because of this reason, brands are fussy about their identities. Many of them have large brand manuals with an exhaustive and exhausting list of what is allowed and what is frowned upon. European engineering brands are the most rigorous in terms of maintaining their identity. I have worked for brands like Philips and Siemens, which have elaborate grids for all their printed material. For example, the Philips grid specifies the height of the letter P of the word Philips to be $(H+W)/10$, where H is the height of the advertisement and W is it's width. Once you calculate the length P, the placement of the logo, the headline, the visual, the baseline etc. are specified in relation to the letter P. No need for an art director here.

The reason for this consistency is that brands are intangible things and the identity helps them to become as familiar as possible. The logic is that consistency helps build trust. Consistency itself is a prerequisite for branding. We often use the word trademark to describe something that is consistent. Thus, Steve Jobs was always to be seen in his 'trademark' black turtleneck, jeans and sneakers.

All this made complete sense when branding was basically for packaged goods and when the printed image was one of the primary means of communication. However, all that is changing fast.

Today, consumers can read. More importantly, the brand may be for a product that has no packaging and the brand graphics do not play a pivotal role. Packaged goods are fussy about things like the dazzle on their pack (Surf) or the striations on the soap (Liril). Those seem superfluous to mobile service operator brands like Vodafone or Airtel.

The strongest brands today are dynamic and playful. Think of Amul. Not only do the topics change, but also the typography of the logo. What does not change is the personality of the brand. Amul is like a witty friend you want to meet regularly to hear her latest witticism about the topic of the day. She likes the same things that we do – movies and cricket - and enjoys them with us. She empathizes when we are sad and she sends out barbs when we are angry. This friend is always lovable and never boring.

Many other brands change their logos consistently too. Google is a familiar example for Internet surfers. People look forward to the Google Doodle of the day and many an hour has been wasted as office workers play with an interactive doodle, or read about the person or event that is commemorated by the doodle.

Similarly, MTV changes its logo often too. MTV's logo changes are often capricious. It changes because someone thought of a cool way to show the logo and not necessarily because of any event.

While I like what Amul, Google and MTV do, my prize for the coolest logo idea goes to an unlikely brand - MIT's Media Lab.

The Wikipedia entry for Media Lab says: "The MIT Media Lab is an interdisciplinary research laboratory at the Massachusetts Institute of Technology devoted to projects at the convergence of technology, multimedia and design." It has been at the forefront of some major advances including the e-ink (on which the Amazon Kindle and other ebook readers are based), MPEG-4 and the technology behind the Google street view maps. Most recently, it has become famous for its 'sixth sense' technology that makes computers adapt to humans rather than force humans to learn to communicate with computers.

I first heard about the Media Lab when I read a book written by its founder director, Nicholas Negroponte, called *Being Digital*. I was struck by the creativity and innovation of their employees.

MIT MEDIA LAB

The logo of Media Lab reflects this creative spirit. The black squares in the logo are the light sources that send out a beam of red, blue or yellow light. These light sources can be placed anywhere on a 9x9x9 matrix, which results in the light streaming out in unique patterns. There are over forty thousand versions of the logo that can be created just by placing the three light sources at different points. Each individual at the Media Lab can choose his or her own version. So each person has a unique logo, while still belonging to the same family.

Brands have come a long way from the days when they were stuck up about the exact Pantone shade of the logo, or the specific way in which their dazzle appeared on the pack.

The question now is whether all brands need to constantly change their logo or not? And how exactly should brands balance change with consistency? Consumers want change because it is fun and not boring. But they also want consistency because they fear too much change. Earlier generations of brand managers responded to these conflicting demands by being rigidly consistent. What should the brand manager of the 21st century do?

From Brand Identity to Brand Experience

"Products are made in the factory, but brands are created in the mind." So said Walter Landor, the man who created the profession of brand identity and founded the design firm Landor Associates. Mr. Landor is credited with having taken the function of label designer and elevated it to a serious profession. He pioneered many techniques of branding and research that are still used today.

Mr. Landor revolutionised packaging design in the fifties in the USA. He recognised the important role that packaging played in making the sale. He famously remarked: "Fifteen years ago, a sales clerk might recommend a brand of soap, paint, peas, or candy. Today, the package itself must do the talking."

One of his most famous designs was for Arrowhead and Puritas of Los Angeles, a leader in bottled water for commercial venues. They wanted to introduce half-gallon glass bottles for the home and restaurant market. Glass containers of this size were unwieldy and heavy, particularly when filled, making them awkward for people seated at a table to lift. The bottle's design had to overcome this difficulty. Mr. Landor and his team created the above design that had two flat surfaces and did not need to be lifted for water to be poured.

Designs such as these are considered classics, but what interests me more is that Mr. Landor's focus was always on the consumer experience. He didn't just design the product label or the packaging, he designed the brand experience. This is the kind of thinking that helped stimulate the consumer movement of the post-World War II era.

This thinking has continued to this day and has become more sophisticated. Today, the entire focus is on consumer experience, almost to the exclusion of the brand logo. Luxury brands like Gucci and Prada have made their logos really small and sometimes remove them altogether from their products leading to an article in The Times, London announcing the 'Death of the Logo'.

A lot of marketers focus on the consistency of their brand colours and the way their logo appears. That emphasis is misplaced. They should focus instead on the consistency of their brand experience. McDonald's is a good example. Their brand experience includes the architecture, uniforms, iconography, event days, clean bathrooms and so on. You know you are in McDonald's even if you don't see the logo.

The metro in Paris was facing losses and wanted a new advertising campaign. The agency they worked with, BETC Euro RSCG, decided that the need was not for a new campaign, but for a new brand experience. Which is what they delivered.

They looked at the entire customer journey, from buying the tickets to waiting on the platforms to the journey itself and then the trip away from the station to their final destination. They did art shows on platforms, created a daily newspaper for reading on the journey, offered bicycles on hire so that you could go from the station to your destination. Every aspect of the experience improved and so did the revenues.

Sometimes, if you get the brand identity absolutely correct, but the brand experience changes, the brand equity changes as well. We saw this in the case of Starbucks. Once the stores smelt of cheese rather than coffee, the brand equity got eroded.

The conclusion is that brand managers need to stop being the policemen of brand identity and start becoming the guardians of brand experience.

ELEPHANT IN THE ROOM:

MARKETING EXPLOITS

MARKETERS MAKE US EAT MORE, BUY MORE, SPEND MORE...
AND NOW THEY WANT TO MAKE US BELIEVE IT IS FOR OUR OWN GOOD?!
BUT YOU CAN'T FOOL ME! NO, SIR! I CAN SEE THROUGH THEIR
LITTLE CON THE CONSUMER GAME! YES, SIR! I CAN SEE.... OH MY!
OOOH! I NEED THAT! I AWAYS WANTED THAT! MUST. BUY. THAT.

Is the Business of Business Only Business?

In the middle of the year 2005, Duncan Goose started a company in the UK called Global Ethics Ltd., which owns the brand 'One'. Unknown to him, a man called Blake Mycoskie discovered a new style of shoe and a new business model on a trip to Argentina. That was in early 2006.

Both these young men started businesses that were very similar in intent. Both are social models that strive to do good in a sustainable manner by running a business.

Blake Mycoskie runs Toms Shoes. For every pair of shoes that a consumer buys, he gifts one pair to a child in need. One for one - a simple but powerful idea. He has been extremely successful and has now extended his product range to include spectacles.

Duncan Goose runs a brand called One. Under this brand, he sells a range of products that include water, eggs, toilet paper, kitchen foil and juice. 100% of the profits from these businesses go to projects that his foundation runs in the needy parts of the world. These projects are mostly in Africa and are mostly related to water.

Both of these are examples of what the Nobel Prize winner, Muhammad Yunus, calls 'Social businesses'. Businesses whose intention is to do good for society. Businesses that don't seek profits for the sake of profits alone. Businesses that could reform capitalism and remove or reduce some of its ills.

Mr. Yunus himself runs several social businesses in Bangladesh. His work has earned him numerous accolades including the Nobel Peace Prize. His businesses use the brand name, Grameen. The starting point for him was the Grameen Bank that pioneered the idea of micro finance. Since then, Grameen has ventured into mobile telephony, energy, textiles, mutual funds, branded yoghurt (in a joint venture with Danone) etc.

Social businesses aren't businesses that also do philanthropy. They are fundamentally different in their approach to business. In this context, it is worth quoting in full an article that is posted on the bank's website - 'Is Grameen Bank Different From Conventional Banks?' Here it is:

"Grameen Bank methodology is almost the reverse of the conventional banking methodology. Conventional banking is based on the principle that the more you have, the more you can get. In other words, if you have little or nothing, you get nothing. As a result, more than half the population of the world is deprived of the financial services of the conventional banks. Conventional banking is based on collateral, Grameen system is collateral- free.

Grameen Bank starts with the belief that credit should be accepted as a human right, and builds a system where one who does not possess anything gets the highest priority in getting a loan. Grameen methodology is not based on assessing the material possessions of a person, it is based on the potential of a person. Grameen believes that all human beings, including the poorest, are endowed with endless potential.

Conventional banks look at what has already been acquired by a person. Grameen looks at the potential that is waiting to be unleashed in a person.

Conventional banks are owned by the rich, generally men. Grameen Bank is owned by poor women.

Overarching objective of the conventional banks is to maximise profit. Grameen Bank's objective is to bring financial services to the poor, particularly women and the poorest - to help them fight poverty, stay profitable and financially sound. It is a composite objective, coming out of social and economic visions.

Conventional banks focus on men, Grameen gives high priority to women. 97% of Grameen Bank's borrowers are women. Grameen Bank works to raise the status of poor women in their families by giving them ownership of assets. It makes sure that the ownership of the houses built with Grameen Bank loans remains with the borrowers, i.e., the women.

Grameen Bank branches are located in the rural areas, unlike the branches of conventional banks that try to locate themselves as close as possible to the business districts and urban centres. First principle of Grameen banking is that the clients should not go to the bank, it is the bank that should go to the people instead. Grameen Bank's 22,124 staff meets 8.35 million borrowers at their door-step in 81,379 villages spread out all over Bangladesh, every week, and deliver bank's service. Repayment of Grameen loans is also made very easy by splitting the loan amount in tiny weekly instalments. Doing business this way means a lot of work for the bank, but it is a lot convenient for the borrowers.

There is no legal instrument between the lender and the borrower in the Grameen methodology. There is no stipulation that a client will be taken to the court of law to recover the loan, unlike in the conventional system. There is no provision in the methodology to enforce a contract by any external intervention.

Conventional banks go into 'punishment' mode when a borrower is taking more time in repaying the loan than it was agreed upon. They call these borrowers 'defaulters'. Grameen methodology allows such borrowers to reschedule their loans without making them feel that they have done anything wrong (indeed, they have not done anything wrong).

When a client gets into difficulty, conventional banks get worried about their money and make all efforts to recover the money, including taking over the collateral. Grameen system, in such cases, works extra hard to assist the borrower in difficulty, and makes all efforts to help them regain their strength and overcome their difficulties.

In conventional banks, charging interest does not stop unless specific exception is made to a particular defaulted loan. Interest charged on a loan can be a multiple of the principal, depending on the length of the loan period. In Grameen Bank, under no circumstances, total interest on a loan can exceed the amount of the loan, no matter how long the loan remains unpaid. No interest is charged after the interest amount equals the principal.

Conventional banks do not pay attention to what happens to the borrowers' families as results of taking loans from the banks. Grameen system pays a lot of attention to monitoring the education of the children (Grameen Bank routinely gives them scholarships and student loans), housing, sanitation, access to clean drinking water, and their coping capacity for meeting disasters and emergency situations. Grameen system helps the borrowers to build their own pension funds, and other types of savings.

Interest on conventional bank loans are generally compounded quarterly, while all interests are simple interests in Grameen Bank.

In case of death of a borrower, Grameen system does not require the family of the deceased to pay back the loan. There is a built-in insurance programme, which pays off the entire outstanding amount with interest. No liability is transferred to the family.

In Grameen Bank, even a beggar gets special attention. A beggar comes under a campaign from Grameen Bank, which is designed to persuade him/her to join Grameen programme. The bank explains to him/her how they can carry some merchandise when they go out to beg from door to door and earn money, or display some merchandise by their side when begging in a fixed place. Grameen's idea is to graduate them to a dignified livelihood rather than continue with begging.

Such a programme would not be a part of a conventional bank's work.

Grameen system encourages the borrowers to adopt some goals in social, educational and health areas. These are known as Sixteen Decisions - no dowry, education for children, sanitary latrine, planting trees, eating vegetables to combat night-blindness among children, arranging clean drinking water, etc.). Conventional banks do not see this as their business.

In Grameen, we see the poor people as human bonsai. If a healthy seed of a giant tree is planted in a flower-pot, the tree that will grow will be a miniature version of the giant tree. It is not because of any fault in the seed, because there is no fault in the seed. It is only because the seed has been denied the real base to grow on. People are poor because society has denied them the real social and economic base to grow on. They are given only the flower-pots to grow in. Grameen's effort is to move them from the flower-pot to the real soil of the society.

If we can succeed in doing that, there will be no human 'bonsai' in the world. We'll have a poverty-free world.

I find this article insightful and inspiring. This is a business that is born of a genuine understanding of its customers. It is a challenger brand that differs dramatically from the leaders in its category. And it is a successful business venture that has grown by leaps and bounds and also spawned a whole lot of other businesses.

Muhammad Yunus is one of the most important reformers of all time. He has shown that businesses can have a heart.

The usual criticism of his model is that it is not really a business. More like an NGO that earns its own money. So let us turn now to how these ideas are changing 'regular' businesses.

Paul Polman and the New Unilever

Paul Polman, the global CEO of Unilever, likes to quote Sir Winston Churchill: "Democracy was the worst form of government apart from all the others that had been tried." Mr. Polman says that capitalism is the worst form of economic organisation except for all the others that have been tried.

The CEO of Unilever says that he is most inspired by people like Gandhi, Mandela and Mother Teresa. That is not unusual. It is quite fashionable these days for leaders to say that they are inspired by great people. What is unusual about Mr. Polman is that he has actual concern for the less fortunate in society and is doing things to make their lives better. In order to do so, he is reinventing his company and perhaps helping capitalism reinvent itself.

The vision that he has set out for his company is so different and refreshing that it is worth reading it. Here is a passage of the vision statement as it appears on the Unilever website:

> "In 2009, we launched what we call 'The Compass' – Unilever's strategy for sustainable growth. It sets out a clear and compelling vision of our future, in which our brands and services reach and inspire people across the world, helping us double the size of our business while reducing our environmental footprint and increasing our positive social impact.

> "It's a goal we're seeking to achieve by developing new ways of doing business through which we can minimise our direct impact and improve hygiene, nutrition, opportunities and health for communities.

> "We're working with our suppliers, consumers and the retailers who sell our brands to improve their sustainability credentials too.

> "By combining our multinational expertise with our deep roots in diverse local cultures, we're continuing to provide a range of products to suit a wealth of consumers. We're also strengthening our strong relationships in the emerging markets we believe will be significant for our future growth.

"And by leveraging our global reach and inspiring people to take small, everyday actions, we believe we can help make a big difference to the world."

These are inspiring words. "Double the size of our business while reducing our environmental footprint and increasing our positive social impact." This is not about doing well at the cost of growth, but doing both together. And Unilever doesn't just want to reduce its own footprint, but that of its entire ecosystem - from its suppliers to itself and on to its consumers.

What is even more inspiring is that the words are followed up with action. We shall read case studies about Unilever brands later. Right now, I just want to focus on the case that Mr. Polman builds for doing this.

The case for change is built on two pillars. The first is that capitalism is leaving too many people behind to be sustainable. According to a new global wealth report published by Credit Suisse Bank and authored by Professors Anthony Shorrocks and Jim Davies, the top 1% of the population owns 41% of the wealth of the world, and the bottom half just owns 1%. This kind of lopsided growth has led to uprisings like the 'Occupy Wall Street' movement. Also, this growth is unsustainable. A study by the WWF, the Zoological Society of London and the Global Footprint Network shows that we are already consuming the resources of one and a half planets and by the year 2030 will need that of two planets. Clearly something needs to be done to change the way we have been growing.

The second is that the power is now in the hands of the consumer. Pointing to what happened in Egypt, he says: "If they could get an entrenched dictatorship out in seventeen days, they can get an irresponsible company out in nanoseconds."

So corporations today have no choice but to create a new business model that is sustainable and responsible. It is not just about corporate social responsibility, but a more integral way of doing business.

According to Mr. Polman, Unilever is trying to do just that.

"If I can achieve a 50% carbon cut in my own shop, that's CSR (corporate social responsibility) at best. If I can achieve a 50% carbon cut in the supply chain, then we can make a ten times bigger impact on the environment.

"Stepping up to the plate is not only the right thing for business to do from a moral perspective, but it is also in our economic self-interest. As CK

Prahalad and others have argued, there are enormous growth and margin opportunities in what people now call 'sustainability'. For Unilever, these are to be found in addressing the needs of billions of people for clean drinking water, basic hygiene and sanitation, nutritious food and sourcing all of our agricultural raw materials sustainably." (http://www.huffingtonpost.com/paul-polman/sustainable-business-wher_b_4064391.html).

All these supply side changes on sourcing make an organisation responsible. But how is it to grow? In order to do that, it needs to ensure that each brand has a social purpose that consumers care about. That social purpose will make the brand more attractive to its consumers and make it grow. Let's turn to some examples now.

Change the World by Washing your Hands

Lifebuoy was launched in the year 1894 by William Lever to combat the cholera epidemic in the UK. Thousands of people were dying due to poor sanitation and this soap brand became a life saver for them. Hence, the name.

Lifebuoy has always been a soap that kills germs and its positioning has been around health. Its jingle is one of the longest running songs in Indian advertising. Most of us (above a certain age) can visualise the stereotypical Lifebuoy film of a sports person falling down in dirt and getting up to win the race. The film is intercut with shots of him bathing with Lifebuoy.

Lifebuoy used to be quite cheap and very effective because it contained carbolic acid. This combination of a good product, low price and impactful advertising made it the world's largest selling soap. In the nineties, the brand started losing customers. Indians were becoming more affluent and they no longer wanted to bathe with bad smelling carbolic soaps. Consumers were moving on to more genteel soaps with brand promises around beauty and fairness. Even when they wanted a health soap, they preferred Dettol with its more premium brand equity.

Lifebuoy went through a phase of confusion as it changed formulations, launched variants and experimented with different advertising platforms. Most of this ended up confusing the audience and Lifebuoy fell way off the top of the mountain of popularity.

So Lifebuoy decided to go back to its roots. Just after the turn of the century, it launched its new positioning with the 'Little Gandhi' commercial. The ad talks about a little boy who decides to clean up the mess on his street all by himself. Other people in the neighbourhood follow his lead and it soon becomes a movement. The message is that only people who are not afraid to fall ill can change the world.

The message that Lifebuoy provides some sort of immunity from illness became the theme of one of the world's largest social campaigns. The campaign, 'Swasthya Chetna' (Health Awakening), educates people on the importance of health and hygiene in preventing diarrhoea and encourages them to adopt a simple hand-washing regime using soap.

Diarrohea is world's leading preventable cause of death, killing over two million people every year including six hundred thousand Indian children under the age of five. According to a study by the London School of Tropical Hygiene, washing hands with soap and water can reduce instances of diarrhoea by 47%.

Lifebuoy health officers visited forty-three thousand Indian villages and schools over a period of five years where they used product demonstrations, interactive visuals, competitions and drama workshops to spread the message of health and hygiene.

The program is based on the simple insight that visible clean is not actual clean, which was brought alive through a special Glo Germ UV demo. When held under ultra-violet lamps, Glo Germ powder glows on hands washed only with water, symbolising germs on those hands, and does not glow on hands washed with soap.

The program has reached one hundred and ten million rural Indians since it began in the year 2002. Awareness of germs has increased by 30% and soap usage has increased by 79% among parents and 93% among children in the targeted areas. Soap consumption has increased by 15%.

This campaign isn't limited just to India. It has spread to several other developing countries including South Africa and Indonesia. Lifebuoy was awarded the title of 'citizen brand' in Indonesia for its work in spreading the idea of hygiene. All this work has once again made Lifebuoy the world's number one health soap.

A good example of combining a social mission with brand growth.

Dovish on Self Esteem

Which of these help women feel more liberated -a bikini or a burqa?

In a speech at the India Today Conclave in New Delhi, a feminist, Germaine Greer, made a strong case to say that a burqa probably gave women more sense of liberty than a bikini. This is a controversial statement, but one that she backed up with logic. So much so that she got a standing ovation at the conclave.

Her logic was that millions of women around the world dread the advent of summers because they would be expected to wear a bikini and they feel that their bodies aren't in good enough shape for that. On the other hand, women who wear burqas don't really have the choice of wearing a bikini. The choice is either to wear the burqa and roam around freely, or not wear it and stay locked up indoors.

According to Unilever, six out of ten girls avoid certain activities because they don't like how they look. Ms Greer wasn't just making a point for the purpose of debate; this is a huge problem and one that is getting exacerbated by the marketing, advertising and media communities.

Dove has set out to tackle this social problem. I want to highlight this brand to show that having a social mission for a brand does not just mean working for the poor. There are other issues that require attention too.

Dove takes an anti-beauty industry stance. It has a film that asks mothers to talk to their daughters before the beauty industry does. It has suggestions for how mothers should talk to their daughters and help them understand the concept of 'real beauty'.

Dove advertisements do not use classical models. Dove has been using real women in advertising since a long time. They have stayed away from the ultra-thin, glamorous, stereotypical look. They promote the idea that real beauty comes from within and could be housed in any body type.

Dove was launched as a soap with moisturising cream that does not make your skin feel dry. This has been promoted by testimonials from real people. These women are not models, but busy housewives or busy career women who have no time for elaborate beauty rituals. Dove is the solution to that problem.

This has morphed into an indictment of the beauty industry. The 'evolution' film went viral on the Internet. This film showed how an ordinary looking woman was transformed into a super model for an advertisement by using post-production techniques like Photoshop. More recently, the 'sketches' film has won a large number of advertising awards and also gone viral. This film cleverly contrasts how women really look versus how they think they look. Most women find faults with themselves, while an objective bystander finds them way more beautiful than they think.

The real benefit of Dove's campaign is that it gives confidence back to women. It doesn't really offer a solution to any problem. The campaign has been criticised for the duplicity of the brand owner, Unilever. The company makes many products that follow the stereotypes of the beauty industry. Products that reinforce the image of the fair, shapely and glamorous woman. While Dove asks women to have confidence in themselves and the way they look, Fair and Lovely suggests that one must be fair to be confident. Critics believe that Dove's campaigns are attempts at manipulating women to get them to buy a product.

Some of that criticism is fair. It is true that Unilever does want to be anti-establishment and pro-establishment at the same time. The only thing we can say is that Dove is an interesting experiment. If it succeeds, the remaining brands will also get off the stereotypical beauty industry bandwagon and that can lead to positive social change.

Meanwhile, women all over the world are watching and sharing Dove videos with each other. It is creating a lot of positive word of mouth for the brand and also helping it grow. It certainly is an unplugged marketing strategy.

Is Doing Good Always Good for Business?

PEPSI REFRESH FROM START TO FINISH

From tagline to grant giver, the highlights (and lowlights)

DECEMBER 2008

Pepsi launches a new tagline, "Every generation refreshes the world," and website, RefreshEverything.com, foreshadowing the Pepsi Refresh Project.

JANUARY 13, 2010

The Pepsi Refresh Project launches, though it's quickly forced to shut down online submissions, due to to technical glitches.

JULY 2010

In response to the Deepwater Horizon water spill, Pepsi pledges $1.3 million to fund ideas to support communities in Gulf states. Major League Baseball teams are also enlisted to compete for a Pepsi Refresh grant.

SEPTEMBER 8, 2010

Pepsi announces it will expand the Pepsi Refresh Project to Europe, Latin America and Asia. Ultimately the program never expanded to those regions.

FEBRUARY 6, 2011

Pepsi is back in the Super Bowl with three 30-second spots for Pepsi Max.

APRIL 28, 2011

Amid criticism that the program isn't driving sales, Pepsi introduces "Power Voting." Codes on Pepsi products allow voters to apply bonus votes to ideas they like.

DECEMBER 2011

Last round of voting closes.

MARCH 2012

RefreshEverything.com goes dark.

DECEMBER 2009

Pepsi says it will sit out the Super Bowl in order to focus on the Pepsi Refresh Project. Consumers can apply for grants ranging from $5,000 to $250,000 in one of six areas: health, arts and culture, food and shelter, the planet and neighborhoods and education. One thousand applications are accepted monthly via refresheverything.com, and consumers vote on the winning projects.

FEBRUARY 2010

For the first time in 23 years, PepsiCo's beverage brands are absent from the Super Bowl broadcast. Pepsi enlists Demi Moore and Kevin Bacon to pitch their own ideas to refresh the world—and generate buzz.

JANUARY 2011

Jan. 5 - The New York Times publishes its investigation into cheating allegations. Pepsi says it is using proprietary methods to identify fraudulent votes.

Jan. 31 - Pepsi makes changes to the program, eliminating the $250,000 grant level and capping grants at $50,000. It also tweaks the grant categories, dropping health, the planet, and food and shelter, while focusing on arts and music, communities and education.

MARCH 17, 2011

Beverage Digest announces Diet Coke has bypassed Pepsi as the nation's No. 2 soda. In 2010, Pepsi's share of the carbonated soft-drink category fell 0.4%, while Diet Pepsi's share fell 0.3%. Shares of both Coke and Diet Coke were flat.

JANUARY 2012

Last round of grants awarded.

Source: Ad Age Blogs, October 8, 2012

Bob Hoffman likes to portray himself as a cranky old man who is exposing the falsehoods of the new gurus of marketing. His book, *101 Contrarian Ideas About Advertising*, has been the best selling advertising book on Amazon. His blog, *The Ad Contrarian*, was named one of the world's most influential advertising and marketing blogs by Business Insider. If he ever reads this book, I am sure he will dismiss it as another example of the new bullshit that just does not work.

For Mr. Hoffman, the Pepsi Refresh project epitomises all the bullshit that the social media proponents and the good-for-business enthusiasts have been proclaiming. The case study also proves that it does not work. He writes, "The Refresh Project accomplished everything a social media program is expected to: Over eighty million votes were registered; almost three point five million 'likes' on the Pepsi Facebook page; almost sixty thousand Twitter followers. The only thing it failed to do was sell Pepsi."

Before I comment on Mr. Hoffman's observations, let us go back and understand the Pepsi Refresh project. The AdAge infographic above does a pretty good job of explaining this and I would urge you to read it fully if you haven't already.

The Pepsi Refresh project was a major initiative of Pepsi's CEO, Indra Nooyi. Ms. Nooyi is one of the most celebrated CEOs in America. After she took over, Pepsi announced that it would not advertise on the Super Bowl and instead the money would be channeled into social projects. Projects that could be submitted and voted on by the general public. This made major news and the marketing world settled down to watch what would happen when a major packaged goods marketer chose social media over conventional media.

The results were great to begin with, but not good in the long run. As Mr. Hoffman says, the project scored well on all the social media metrics, but not in sales. Two years after launching it, the project was withdrawn and Pepsi went back to advertising on the Super Bowl. The failure of the Refresh campaign has also been a setback for Ms. Nooyi who is said to be under pressure from her board and shareholders since the campaign failed to deliver.

So what can we learn from this case study? Why did Pepsi fail? There is a very interesting blog post on the subject written by Craig Bida, executive vice president of cause branding and nonprofit marketing for Cone

Communications, a public relations and marketing agency. He writes:

> "From a strategic perspective, the program's end is no surprise. Unfocused models like the Pepsi Refresh Project are generally ineffective in engaging stakeholders, optimising business and social impact, and building equity. Though innovative (crowd-sourced voting) and relevant (tapping into increasing consumer appetite for cause), the Pepsi Refresh Project was flawed from the outset. Here's why:

1. With so many nonprofits participating in the voting program, it was nearly impossible to vet all organisations thoroughly, resulting in persistent allegations of fraud.
2. The pressure on nonprofits to tap supporters for votes became a significant resource drain, causing some organisations to withdraw.
3. Not having a direct product tie-in decreased odds from the start that this would drive sales - a big no-no in a declining and fiercely competitive category.
4. Supporting multiple organisations across multiple issues/geographies led to scattered results, versus a concentrated impact on a specific issue.
5. Finally, when it comes to causes, if you don't stand for something, you stand for nothing. Despite millions of dollars in grants (estimated at $25 million), it's hard to articulate what the program was really about and where real results could be found, beyond broad generosity."

To me, the most damning criticism of the points above is that the project stood for nothing. As Mr. Bida says, "If you don't stand for something, you stand for nothing." This is the big difference from the Lifebouy and Dove campaigns that we have seen earlier.

The Pepsi Refresh model was replicated almost exactly in India by the auto giant, Mahindra. They called their programme 'Rise', which was also their new corporate tagline. Apart from a few details, this campaign copied Pepsi's Refresh campaign both in terms of the way it was executed and also in the kind of results that it achieved.

I spoke to a person who is part of the corporate branding team at Mahindra. He told me that the campaign did do well for the brand equity of Mahindra though not for the sales of its products.

Two case studies that show that vaguely doing good for society is not good enough for a brand. It seems too much like the brand is trying to gain from doing philanthropy and does not seem to be a new way of doing business. Consumers are smart enough to see through this.

ELEPHANT IN THE ROOM:

DON'T FOLLOW INDUSTRY BEST PRACTICES

To Copy is Human

Bollywood is good at following the money.

In the seventies, Hindi filmmakers discovered a nice formula to make money. The movies of that period were romantic movies with great songs and happy endings. The story always revolved around a boy and a girl from different backgrounds, who fell in love and tried to overcome fierce resistance from their families and lecherous villains. Ultimately, they prevail in a tear-jerking climax. If the producer of the movie could get Rajesh Khanna to act in the movie and Kishore Kumar to sing the songs, then he could laugh all the way to the bank.

In the eighties, the formula changed. The villains evolved from being lecherous and muscular to rich and powerful egomaniacs with huge private armies. The focus of the villain was no longer to get the girl, but to inflict some terrible injustice on society as a whole. Along came the hero from a humble background. He could fight an entire army with his bare hands and win. The love interest was still there, but was no longer the subject of the film. The songs were no longer soulful ditties, but had evolved into pulsating dance numbers and folksy sing-alongs. This is the era when Amitabh Bachchan literally stood tall.

In the nineties, the formula changed again with the advent of Shahrukh Khan. Now the anti-hero evolved. He was no longer all good or poor. He combined aspects of the villain in his own persona.

In each era, there have been just one or two pioneering movies that set up the formula and everyone else followed the leader. The first movie with a successful new formula would, by definition, be a hit. This would be followed by a couple of other hits. Some of these might even be bigger than the first as the formula got perfected. Then the later followers made less and less money, until the formula had lost all its money making potential and the industry was ready for a whole new blueprint.

Perhaps, you aren't surprised that Bollywood copies so many formulae. After all, it is run by businessmen who are primarily in it for money. So it is not surprising that they overrule the creative types and insist on playing safe.

The surprising thing is that even when creative people are not being dictated to by hard hearted businessmen, they still choose to follow the leader. Look at the realm of painting, for example. We can study the evolution of painting in Europe from the renaissance period and see how the 'fashions' changed even in art.

The renaissance period lasted for around three centuries and is characterised by the use of perspective, the study of human anatomy and proportion, and the development of an unprecedented refinement in drawing and painting techniques. This period gave way to the Baroque period, which is characterised by great drama, rich, deep colour, and intense light and dark shadows. Baroque art was meant to evoke emotion and passion instead of the calm rationality that had been prized during the Renaissance.

The Baroque period was followed by Rococo, Neo-classicism, Romanticism, Impressionism, Symbolism and other schools of art. It seems that if you lived in a certain period and wanted to be a successful artist, you had to follow the creative style of that period. It is very difficult to break out and start a new style.

The question facing the artists was whether they wanted to be successful or wanted a permanent place in history. If the latter, then you were well advised to create your own new style. The artists we remember are the people who made the new breakthroughs and helped to create new schools of art.

Same is true for marketing. It is easy to copy a successful player in the market. If you are quick enough, then you will even make money. However, as time goes on, following the leader pays less and less dividends and the pressure mounts to create a new path - to challenge the leader and then lead another category.

In times gone by, the pressure to change built up slowly. Categories didn't evolve very fast. Today that has changed. The half-life period of categories is very short and the time between a leader creating a new category and the formula running out of steam is very short. Today, the pressure to innovate is higher than ever before.

Adam Morgan wrote a book called *Eating the Big Fish* where he argues that challenger brands need to think in different ways from leaders. That seems obvious, but unfortunately, most literature on marketing and business focus on case studies of market leaders and expects everyone to learn from them. Yet, the big money is to be made only when you challenge the leaders. Let's look at a few examples.

Everybody Loves the Underdog

Everybody loves the underdog. And we get thrilled when, against all odds, the underdog wins.

In early 2008, Barrack Obama had become the frontrunner in the election race to become the Democratic Party candidate and later the President. This was not a position he wanted to be in and so he insisted: "I'm always the underdog."

In American elections, the underdog always gets the sympathy and support of the media. This lasts until he becomes the favourite, at which time he becomes the target of media's attacks. Clearly, Mr. Obama understood that it is better to be the underdog for as long as possible.

Cinema is full of stories about the underdogs winning. Amitabh Bachchan played the angry young man in countless movies, fighting against the powerful forces of the establishment and winning eventually. We cheered for him each time. Before him, Dilip Kumar and Rajesh Khanna also became superstars while playing underdog roles.

Hollywood is full of underdog stories too. From Rocky, Indiana Jones, Norma Rae Webster to Hans Solo, Oskar Schindler and Erin Brockovich, they're all underdogs that are greatly admired.

Charlie Chaplin was always the underdog. Would we have loved him as much if instead of 'The Little Tramp' he played 'The Bloated Plutocrat'?

In real life, underdogs often lose. That doesn't prevent us from loving them and wiping off a tear when they finally lose. All that we want is for them to put up a really good fight. It happens in sports all the time. The entire crowd gets behind the lower ranked team or the weaker player and often motivates them into playing well above their best. And we absolutely love it when the underdog takes over the champion or scores a goal against the run of play.

In marketing too, it pays to be the underdog. Avis became a likeable brand because it told everyone that it was the small guy compared to Hertz, and therefore tried harder. Pepsi revels in its role as the challenger to big brand

Coke. It keeps up that role even in countries like India where it is way bigger than Coke!

While we like to watch underdogs fight champions, we ourselves would much rather be the champions. This is human nature. The only problem is that when you have reached the top, the only way you can go is down. Perhaps, it is best to be like Mr. Obama and keep thinking and believing that you are the underdog.

HMT was the dominant market leader in watches in India. Indians at that time typically owned a single watch and this was usually received as a gift at major events such as weddings or on passing out of school. HMT watches were sturdy and were treated like heirlooms. Hand-me-downs were quite common. Around 5% of the range at this time comprised of quartz watches - the rest were mechanical and automatic.

Enter Titan. Titan was dramatically different from HMT in almost every respect. It only offered quartz watches. These had beautifully designed faces. They were sold from exclusive stores as well as from unconventional watch outlets such as consumer durable stores. Most of all, Titan focused on getting the consumers to treat a watch as a fashion accessory rather than as a utilitarian device. They encouraged gifting and suggested that everyone needed to have several watches.

Titan did not do this by accident. It deliberately went about breaking all the conventions of the category. On its website, Titan identifies five conventions that they broke:

- Mechanical watches were the norm and they were a full quartz range with a focus on accuracy.
- Styling was basic, while Titan decided to 'make style a table stake'.
- Choice was limited. Typically, the consumer had two hundred models to pick from and these weren't refreshed regularly. Titan started with three hundred and fifty models and then kept adding to this range with newer and newer designs and sub ranges.
- Shops were dark, dingy and uninteresting. So Titan brought about a mini retailing revolution in terms of the design of their showrooms, the quality of the merchandising, the width of the network (later became the world's largest network of watch stores) and by locating their stores within easy browsing reach of the consumer.
- Advertising was expenditure, whereas Titan saw it as a vital investment and swamped the consumer with ads.

All these dramatic changes were captured and summarised by the music track that Titan has used from the very beginning. It was taken from the third movement of Mozart's 25th symphony in G minor. The track was rendered in new instruments that Mozart would not have even heard of. To quote the Titan website again:

"The music was singularly appropriate: it exuded enthusiasm and energy, flamboyance and power, tenacity and triumph. It was young and full of zest, typical of the composer himself. Yet it was classy and elegant. And, of course, it was very European. Both the music and the man who wrote it, perhaps the greatest musical genius of all time, had all the right connotations and fitted so very well with the character of the brand and of the organisation that we were seeking to create."

The results were epic. The public sector players - HMT and Allwyn - were soon driven out of the market. The entire market moved to quartz and Titan has been the dominant market leader in watches ever since.

Guru-speak: Eating the Big Fish

Every industry and category has only one leader and many challengers or underdogs. By the sheer logic of numbers, most of us will work for challenger companies rather than for the leaders. Yet, all business books use leader brands as case studies and seem to focus on them. One book that does not do so is *Eat the Big Fish* by Adam Morgan.

Mr. Morgan set out to analyse challenger brands and work out what makes them successful. The principles or credos that he sets out in his book are good principles to not just help a challenger brand become a leader, but also stay a leader once it gets to that position.

He has three criteria to define a successful challenger brand. The first is the state of the market. Obviously, challenger brands do not have the highest market share. The second is the state of mind. Successful challenger brand realise that their ambitions are greater than their resources and are prepared to work with this reality. The third is that they have high momentum. Successful challenger brands may be smaller than the leader, but they are moving up faster than the leader. And they are doing so in a profitable way.

Challenger brands create a strong momentum by becoming thought leaders. That is the core idea of this book. Market leaders try to maintain the status quo because that favours them. If there is change, they like to manage it and allow changes to occur only gradually. Challenger brands need to create sudden disruptions in the market and accelerate change. In order to do so, they need to create a new idea and over deliver on it.

Some of the ideas in this book are parallel to the ideas in the book *Blue Ocean Strategy*. Both essentially focus on not fighting the battle that your competitor is currently winning, but create a new battlefield altogether. It's back again to ideas, to creativity, to gut-feel and letting go of predictable, safe options.

Adam Morgan has eight credos that challenger brands need to live by. He has divided these credos into four stages.

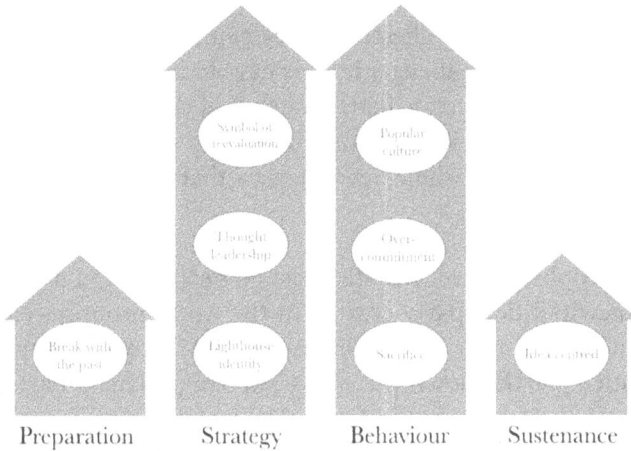

	Symbol of reevaluation	Popular culture	
	Thought leadership	Over-commitment	
Break with the past	Lighthouse identity	Sacrifice	Idea centred

| Preparation | Strategy | Behaviour | Sustenance |

The first stage is of attitude. It's the attitude of the company and the people that make the company. I often find that people who have been doing very well in leading companies in their industry, do very badly when they leave their original employers and join a smaller player. Perhaps, this is because they are not able to make the mental shift between working for a leader and working for a challenger brand. This usually has little to do with the actual content of the work, and everything to do with the mindset.

The second stage is that of the actual strategy. This is the basic idea of the book that challenger brand strategy needs to be very different from that of the leaders. Obviously, a me-too strategy is not going to create disruption in the category.

The third stage is about behaviour. Having created a differentiated strategy, it is over to the execution. The actual performance on the ground needs to be aligned to the strategy and should even develop it further.

Finally, the fourth stage is of sustaining the momentum. Having reached a stage where the challenger brand is seen as a thought leader (or perhaps even a market leader), how does it continue with the good work? What can it do to prevent itself from being eaten up by other smaller fishes?

Titan epitomises several of the credos of Adam Morgan's challenger brands.

The first credo is: Break with the immediate past.

This is the only credo in the first stage. Challenger brands are about discontinuity and change. Therefore, they cannot appear to be similar to the old, even if better. Challenger brands have to be dramatically different. Titan did not try to just create better watches of the type that were already available and sell them in the same outlets to the same consumers. It innovated and created a whole new category that ultimately swamped the old one.

This seemingly obvious credo is often lost on people. I find it very amusing that every new political party created in the world promises change, and even revolution. Yet, they all call themselves the 'People's Party'. Think of Indian political parties down the ages - Jan Sangh, Janata Party, Bhartiya Janata Party, Lok Dal, Rashtriya Janata Dal and Bahujan Samaj Party. All these names are variations on the theme of 'Indian People's Party'.

This is true not just of India. The leading political party in Pakistan is Pakistan People's Party. In Bangladesh, it is the Awami League, which also means people's party. One of Spain's most popular parties is called 'Partido Popular' - by now I don't have to provide the translation.

If all these parties are about change, then surely they can start by changing the naming convention.

This happens in categories other than politics too. Most brand names have a similar sound or a similar meaning or a similar structure. For example, the three leading television networks in the USA were called ABC, NBC and CBS. The fourth channel that started decided to call itself FBS. A perfect case of following the leader. Later, better sense prevailed and FBS changed its name to Fox. Doesn't that sound refreshingly different? More on this later.

Many brands try to change their name, their logo and their colours in order to look new. Obviously, these companies have taken the first credo to heart, and that is a good thing. However, some of these brands don't make real changes from the past. Consumers have understood this and have now become cynical about these cosmetic changes.

Apple is a good example of a company that constantly breaks with its own past and that of the categories that it is entering. The iPhone did not look like any other phone in the market and the iPad does not look like any other net-book in the market.

This credo is about more than just symbolism. This is about the mindset of doing something different. A mindset that is creative and inventive. However, sometimes this may happen because the leader has used his market power to block the normal channels of doing business. Titan, for example, had problems selling its watches through the existing watch dealers. These dealers were loyal to HMT and probably did not buy into the new fangled strategy of Titan anyway. Therefore, Titan was forced to be innovative in its distribution strategy.

The second stage is about challenger strategy and there are three credos here, which are:

- Build a lighthouse identity
- Assume thought leadership of the category
- Create symbols of re-evaluation

Lighthouse identity is all about standing for something sharp and well defined. There is far too much clutter in today's world for us to be able to focus on brands that are only a shade better than another. Such shade differences blur into one. According to Adam Morgan, we need to have brands that are distinctly positioned and have a strong sense of who they are. I would like to add that brands need to be clear about the cause they stand for.

Lighthouse brands need to be obsessed by something. That obsession becomes the sharp edge of the wedge and helps to distinguish the brand from all the others in the category -to stand out from the blur.

Apple is obsessed by design. Apple's CEO, Steve Jobs, hated buttons and loved sleek looks. Each Apple product sets new standards in product design.

Oakley's CEO says, "Product obsession is primary." Nike certainly is obsessed by their products. They almost missed the fact that shoes are about fashion too, since they were so focussed on producing the most high performance shoe for every sport.

The Body Shop founder, Anita Roddick, was obsessed with ethical consumerism. So her brand stood for fair trade with third world countries and no testing on animals.

Ratan Tata was obsessed with low cost and reinvented car manufacturing so that they could produce the Nano for INR 1 lakh. His obsession for low cost seems to go beyond cars. The mobile phone services from Tata group have set new benchmarks for low cost in the industry. Similarly, another Tata group company, Voltas, produces air conditioners priced under INR 10,000, which is also a new low.

It is interesting to note that brands that have a strong lighthouse identity also have a CEO who is closely identified with the business. I guess obsession is a human trait and has to flow through the organisation from the top.

The second credo is the most important credo of the book. If you have to be a successful challenger brand then you need to be a thought leader. You need to do something that makes consumers sit up and take notice. That is the only way.

The Bhartiya Janata Party (BJP) had become an irrelevant party in India having won only two seats in the Lok Sabha elections of the year 1984. Yet, by the mid nineties, it had become the reference point for Indian politics. Every other party's position was defined with reference to that of the BJP. Finally, it came to power in the year 1996 and then again in the year 1998 for a short while. Finally, it won a resounding majority in the 1999 elections and ruled for a full five-year term. Currently, it is in power at the centre again.

The Congress party has traditionally been the thought leader in India. It was the party that won us independence and then ruled the country without a break for the first thirty years. In fact, over the sixty years of the nation's existence, the Congress has ruled at the center for a total of fifty years. Yet, the BJP managed to beat this heavyweight and take center stage for a decade.

What happened to propel a marginalized party into the most important one of the country?

Simply put, it took on the plank of Hindutva. All other parties used the same old cliches about socialism and secularism. The BJP decided to go against that grain and spoke up against what it called 'pseudo secularism'. It made the Ayodhya temple the focal point of its campaign and conducted a Rath Yatra across the country to galvanise support for its cause. Now everyone had to decide whether they were pro Hindutva or against it. The BJP managed to successfully grab thought leadership on the Indian political scene.

Whether you believe in the Hindutva philosophy or not, you have to admit that this is an amazing example of good marketing. It systematically ticks off all the boxes for a challenger brand. It does this on a large scale - a nation of over a billion people with an electorate of over seven hundred million. It did this over a good length of time - a decade. Clearly, thought leadership is not only a niche strategy for premium brands, but can be a mass strategy for all kinds of brands too.

There are many examples of conventional brands taking on the leaders in their categories by seizing thought leadership.

Every category has its traditional way of doing business, which may have been relevant at a particular point in time. However, these practices are not always updated as technologies, consumer expectations and other factors change. This is what gives challenger brands the opportunity to take thought leadership.

A good case in point is the airlines business. Most airlines have developed a hub and spoke network to service passengers. They have competed on the basis of flying to a larger list of destinations, providing good service on board and pampering their business class passengers who are their most profitable customers.

The game changers in this field were the discount airlines led by South West Airlines in the USA, and Ryanair and Easyjet in Europe. They flew only point to point. They had just one class in the plane and did not serve free food or drinks on it. They offered no frequent flyer miles, nor did they sell tickets through travel agents. They did not even provide assigned seating on the aircraft.

But they did provide extremely low fares and even offered money back for delays. Thus, they catered to a new kind of traveller - the entrepreneur rather than the company man. This entrepreneur cared more for the savings rather than for the perks of travel. The larger airlines had ignored this customer.

TV network business in the USA was similar. As already mentioned, the leaders were ABC, NBC and CBS. Prime time programming at this time consisted of a steady diet of soap operas and sitcoms. These had done well over the years, but were now becoming predictable and boring. The fourth network to enter was Fox Broadcasting Service or FBS. After a few years of trying to produce 'better' programming and beating the competition at its own game, it decided to go radical. It changed its name to Fox and brought in a line up of unusual programming. A science fiction based detective show called The X Files; an animated show for adults called The Simpsons; and a crime based reality show called America's Most Wanted.

The last credo in this section is about creating a symbol of re-evaluation. That symbol is like a flag that everyone can rally around. The flag is a symbol of the nation. Similarly, brands need to have a symbol that they can run up a flagpole.

For Fox, it was the change in the name. For the BJP, it was the Rath Yatra.

The fastest growing chain of mid priced hotels in India is called Lemon Tree. The chain has an avant-garde attitude that they believe reflects that of their customers. Most of their employees wear their hair in a ponytail with a yellow bow around it. Just their way of saying, and reminding us, that they are different.

This symbol is crucial because it becomes the talking point for Prosumers. When I talk about the hairstyle of the employees at Lemon Tree, I also talk about the hotel and end up spreading the word about it. This is great publicity for the chain at very little cost.

Similarly, Richard Branson is able to create lots of publicity by his antics that always keep the Virgin brand in news. Whether it is arriving on board the first Virgin aircraft into India dressed like a Maharaja, or trying to cross the Pacific in a hot air balloon, Mr. Branson is always in the news.

The third stage of being a challenger brand is the actual execution or behaviour. This stage again has three credos:

- Sacrifice
- Over commitment
- Using advertising to enter popular culture

The third one sounds a bit self-serving coming from someone who works in the advertising industry (both Adam Morgan and I). So I shall not stress on that too much! Let's talk instead of the other two credos, which are related.

In their book, *Blue Ocean Strategy*, the authors made the point that brands need to go below industry standard in some areas and even eliminate some features. Just so that they can go way above industry standards in other features and invent new ones. The same point is being made here. You need to choose your battles. Then put all your resources into that battle, while withdrawing them from other places.

Market leaders tend to be all things to all people. Challenger brands cannot do so. They simply do not have the resources or the credibility to do so. Hence, they have to sacrifice some segments of the market, perhaps.

The discount airlines sacrifice the business traveller so that they can focus on the entrepreneur. Fox sacrificed the hardcore soap opera fans so that they could capture a larger share of the others.

An outstanding case in point is that of chocolates in the UK in the sixties and early seventies. At that time (and probably even now), 85% of all chocolates were consumed by children. However, Rowntree decided to launch a product aimed at adults. The brand they launched was called 'After eight' and was a runaway success. So much so that it became the overall market leader in the fragmented category, even though it had sacrificed most of the market and over committed to just one small segment of the market. The brand focused on gracious dinner parties and continues to be deliberately exclusive. Probably makes a lot of children hanker for it even though they don't particularly like the taste.

Challenger brands need to make the best use of their resources. Sun Tzu would have advised them that the only way to win the battle is to throw more resources at it than your opponent. The only way to do this is to be selective about your battles.

Yet marketers are always in a hurry to go national or reach out to all segments of the market or cater to all users. I guess that is why so many fail in establishing new brands.

The fourth and the last stage is about sustaining the momentum.

It is a truism that the very factors that help a brand become a leader also cause its downfall. The CEO of Intel, Andy Grove, wrote a book called *Only the Paranoid Survive*. This book should be mandatory reading for CEOs of leading companies.

Leaders are usually displaced by the player that the leader least expects to be a threat.

Surf was the market leader in detergents almost from the day it was born for the next two decades. Then a little upstart company called Nirma came and upset the status quo. It had a product that was produced with low capital investment, had low quality but very low price. Nirma attracted consumers who had never used detergents before into the category. But it also attracted Surf users to downgrade, at least for some of their needs.

There was no way that the managers at Hindustan Lever (the owners of the Surf brand) would have heeded the threat from a little known player from Gujarat. They were more focussed on the larger corporates. But the large companies played by the same rules as Hindustan Lever and posed no threat. Only a player who thought differently could upset a Goliath.

This story of David and Goliath has been told and retold numerous times and in countless ways. In mythology, in cinema and in sports. Often, these stories are told as stories of valour and courage. They are actually stories of creativity - of doing something that the leader did not expect and putting all of one's energy into just that.

The leader has no choice but to be paranoid about everybody. Especially in today's environment where technology is changing the whole competitive landscape. Camera brands are being threatened by mobile phone brands and music labels have discovered that their largest retailers are mobile service operators.

The interplay between product brands and the retail brand is interesting. Most retail brands are built due to the product brands that they carry. They need the support of the product brands to build their business. Yet, as they grow larger, they tend to reduce the strength of the very same product brands.

Departmental stores have reduced the power of readymade brands. We now prefer to go to Shopper's Stop rather than the Arrow showroom to buy our shirts. Once there, we may pick up a shirt that is different from the brand we went to buy.

Consumer durable chains do the same thing. Vijay Sales is the dominant retailer of consumer electronics in Bombay. I identify myself as a Vijay Sales customer and not as a Samsung or a Philips one even though I have bought their products. When I need a new TV, I go to Vijay Sales and end up buying the brand that they push at me. When I have a problem with it, I call up Vijay Sales and they make sure a company technician comes around on the double. In fact, if I call up the company service center, the response is often more sluggish than if I go via the retailer. No wonder my loyalties are more to the trader than to the manufacturer.

It is, however, not easy to stay paranoid. Human beings assume that the current state of affairs will last for a long time, if not forever. Change is always seen as an enemy and hence undesirable. Creating change deliberately is difficult.

The iconic CEO of GE, Jack Welch said: "If we don't systematically destroy our own business, our competitors will." Do we have the courage to do so?

The Quest for an Opposition Party in India

The Indian National Congress is the party that won India its independence from the British. It was so closely aligned with the idea of India, that its flag became the inspiration for the national flag. Before independence and for a few decades more, Congress truly was India.

So how do you go about creating a challenger brand to the Congress?

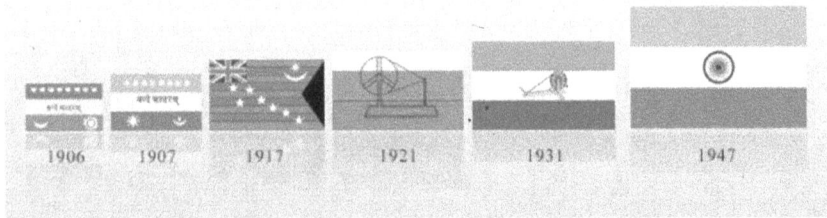

If you opposed the Congress party, you practically opposed the idea of India. Parties that broke away from the Congress retained the ideology of the party and even tried to stay close to the name. The original split in the party took place in the year 1967 and the two factions became Congress (O) and Congress(R). Later on, the latter turned into the present Congress (I).

Other breakaways were more interesting. Jagjiwan Ram started a party in the year 1997 called Congress for Democracy. Today's key offshoots are the Rashtrawadi Congress Party of Sharad Pawar, the Trinamool Congress of Mamata Bannerjee, the YSR Congress of Jaganmohan Reddy, the Haryana Janhit Congress and the Kerala Congress. In all, there are ninety-nine parties registered with the Election Commission that have the word 'Congress' in their name.

In the year 1977, all the opposition parties in the country united to become the Janata Party. This was the first true opposition party in India and it came to power in the elections held that year. Yet, this party's defining ideology can best be described as being 'anti-Congress'. It really had nothing else to hold it together and so it disintegrated within three years. In any case, the policies of the Janata Party were remarkably similar to those of the Congress, and several of its leaders were ex-Congressmen.

So, while the Janata Party was the first nationally successful opponent of the Congress, it was not really a challenger brand.

The national discourse was set by the Congress, and everyone else talked around it.

That was until the Bhartiya Janata Party (BJP) came along. Actually, even the BJP was not a truly challenger brand from the moment of its inception. It acquired that status only after LK Advani's Rath Yatra and the Ayodhya Mandir movement.

The BJP started out to be completely different from the Congress. All along, the grand old party of India had prided itself for being a secular and socialist party. The BJP called it 'pseudo-secular' and suggested that it was pandering to the minorities for political purposes. Suddenly, people all over the country started debating the idea of secularism and the BJP led the debate.

Also, in the seventies and eighties, the country had performed badly on the economic front and people were beginning to get disillusioned with the socialist policies of the Congress. The BJP positioned itself as the right wing, business friendly party and took the lead on this parameter as well.

Finally, the Congress had acquired a reputation for nepotism and self-serving leaders. The BJP projected its disciplined cadres and suggested that it was a more honest party with real leaders who had worked themselves up the hard way.

Many of these values of the BJP are embedded in our current Prime Minister, Narendra Modi. He is the blue-eyed boy of the RSS who has risen from a humble background. He has been a successful Chief Minister of Gujarat for three terms and is loved by the business community. He is seen as being fiercely pro-Hindu, though he seems to be trying to tone down that aspect of his image.

While the BJP continues to lead the debate among mainstream political parties, a rank outsider has emerged to steal the limelight. This is the Aam Aadmi Party (AAP). It projects itself as the anti-politics political party. Their leaders talk about a new kind of politics that is based on honesty and integrity and focused on the needs of the common people rather than the politicians themselves.

AAP has listed all sources of its funds on its website and also stopped accepting more funds once it had collected INR 20 crores. Never before has a political party been so transparent and never before has a party said that it doesn't need more money to fight an election. These actions immediately became a somatic marker for the party.

The Congress party has been the established party for governance in India from the first ever elections in the country. Now it is being challenged by new parties and is in danger of being marginalised forever. Whatever happens to politics in India, it is certainly an interesting case study for students of challenger brands.

ELEPHANT IN THE ROOM:

BRANDS ARE MORE IMPORTANT THAN EVER

Is the Brand Dead or Merely Critically Ill?

Remember Akai TV? If you are too young to remember, let me tell you the story.

Kabir Mulchandani disrupted the colour TV industry in the mid 1990s. Mr. Mulchandani was a Stanford University dropout who wore incredibly expensive Armani suits and sold incredibly cheap television sets. He was very successful for a while. In just a year and a half, he grabbed 18% market share and became the poster boy of the new India in that era. He competed against established brands like Sony, Panasonic, Philips, BPL, Videocon and Onida. For a while, it looked like he was winning. The fairy tale didn't last, but the Prince did make a lasting impact on marketing in India.

Kabir Mulchandani launched a brand called 'Akai' in India. He didn't bother to build the brand in any conventional way, and instead launched his brand with a series of price ads. Kabir's insight was that Indians did not like to throw away anything and so he introduced the concept of exchange offers. His ads offered a new price point of INR 9,999 for a 21 inch TV set (as against a minimum of INR 15,000 for the competition) if you bought an Akai in exchange for any brand of TV. Mr. Mulchandani also pioneered the idea of launching advertisements before the products were displayed in the showrooms, thus using mass media to create a distribution network. The brand also offered outrageous incentives to dealers to sell Akai. I worked on the Philips brand at that time and Akai really had us and all other competitors on the run.

Akai was the first truly discounted brand in India. One can argue that there had always been cheap brands in every category. Some of them, like Nirma detergent powder, had also been very successful. But those products were seen by consumers as being inferior to the standard products. Typically, the cheaper product also looked cheap. So the association in the consumers' minds was clear - cheap brands were of inferior quality.

Akai was different. Here was a Japanese brand selling a product that seemed as good or even better than the competition. And it was being sold at a price that was less than a third of others. Suddenly, the idea that standard brands cost money was seriously challenged.

Akai not only changed the way consumers durables were sold in India, it also changed the equation that consumers have with brands. One of the roles that a brand plays is to provide consistency of pricing and quality. Now consumers realised that similar products could have widely varying prices. Akai itself sold at different prices on different days and in different outlets. The sanctity of brands was under threat.

This brand erosion has happened in other places too. In the USA, car brands started discounting themselves badly. The consumer could get the same car at different prices from different dealers. Moreover, the dealers started offering 'sticker prices' that were shockingly low, but accessories costed extra. These accessories often included critical components of the car and so consumers couldn't really compare prices. It became so bad that a new car brand, Saturn, initially started to do well merely because it brought in a one-price policy across its distribution network.

This has got worse with the advent of retail brands. The consumer durables retail chain, Croma, offers 'Croma' brand products at vastly lower prices than the competing product made by a multinational brand that is sold alongside in the same aisle. This trend is really prevalent in the developed markets where private label brands are sold at half the price of the better known brands.

There is a new breed of hyper-informed super-consumers out there who know exactly what it costs to manufacture a product. There are websites that inform consumers about what it costs to make the products. These consumers also know all the tricks of marketing. They know how much celebrities are paid to endorse brands, they have found ways to skip advertisements and they communicate good and bad news to each other through social media.

There is also an explosion of brands today. Earlier, each category would have one dominant leader, one or two strong challengers and then a few smaller, niche brands. That's all gone now. Now each category is fragmented with dozens of brands fighting for share. There are rarely any clear leaders and consumers get confused about what to buy.

In an article, *The Decline of Brands*, James Surowiecki says:

> "Marketers may consider the explosion of new brands to be evidence of branding's importance, but in fact, the opposite is true. It would be a waste of money to launch a clever logo into a world of durable

brands and loyal customers. But because consumers are more promiscuous and fickle than ever, established brands are vulnerable and new ones have a real chance of succeeding - for at least a little while. The obsession with brands, paradoxically, demonstrates their weakness."

Mr. Surowiecki goes on to say that consumers' expectations have been raised so high that even brands that offer excellent quality and service are unable to get loyalty for any sustained length of time. He calls this the 'What Have You Done for Me Lately?' economy.

So a combination of rash marketers, knowledgeable consumers and raised expectations have resulted in an erosion of brand loyalty. There was a time when a loyal consumer was one who used a certain brand of soap seven times out of ten. Today, the standard for loyalty has dropped to three out of ten and even then the percentage of loyal consumers is at an abysmally low level.

What now? Is the era of brands over? Should we say that we are now moving into an era of near perfect competition where consumers have perfect information, evaluate products on the basis of features and price and buy the one with the best value or is that a utopian state? Do brands still have a role to play?

A New Model for Brands

When I first learnt of brands, I was told that a brand could be visualised as a ball with an inner core and an outer covering. The inner core contained the rational propositions of the brand - what it does, how much it costs etc. The outer layer is the emotional connections that a brand makes with its consumers - how it makes consumers feel.

Over time, the relative importance of the two layers changes. When a category is new, most brands in it would be 'reference brands'. Utility companies like Reliance Power are an example of reference brands. They have a name and they have consumer benefits, but very little emotional connect with the user. Later brands develop into 'personality brands' that compete on the basis of the emotional connections they forge with consumers. For example, most packaged goods like Dove, Maggi and Ariel fall in this category. Finally, some brands attain the status of 'icon brands' where the emotional connections overshadow the product attributes. A good example is of Harley Davidson in motorcycles.

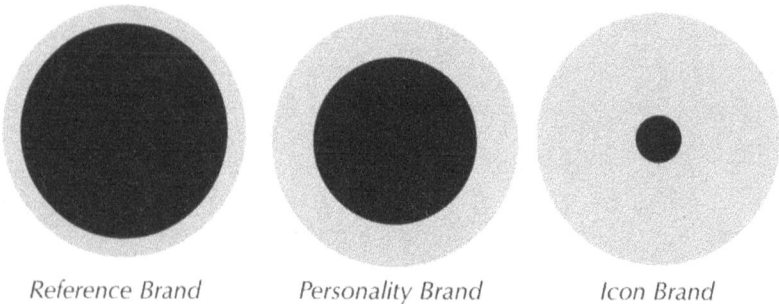

Reference Brand   *Personality Brand*   *Icon Brand*

This model of brands has worked well for several decades. It has worked particularly well in the era of mass media and at a time when most 'brands' sold packaged goods. But in the light of everything we have discussed in this book, this model needs to change.

At the very least, we now need three facets rather than just two. Along with the rational proposition and the emotional connect, we need to add a third facet related to social value. The strongest brands are the brands that give people a sense of belonging to a community. Defining what social value a brand provides would be a valid third leg for the brand.

We now have a triangle where the three corners describe the key elements of a brand. However, even this is not satisfactory since we know that consumers aren't rational. Also, maybe we ought to get culture into brand definition. Also, since we know that people talk about a brand if they have a great experience, we should define that as well. Hence, we now get a very new triangle as shown below.

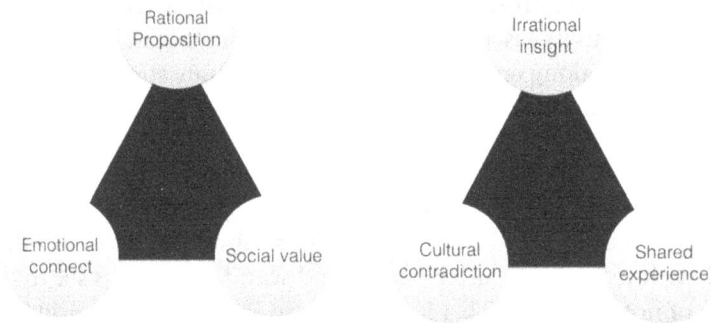

This new triangle can be the basis of how we define brands. Let's take an example to understand how this works.

Nike is a brand that is close to my heart. And it is also a well-established global brand. The Indian Premier League (IPL) is a new brand that is already highly valued. Let us see how well this new model works for both these brands.

Nike's insight seems to be that deep down many of us believe that we are good athletes. Either we were good once, or we could become good, or we could have been good if only we had the right opportunities.

The cultural contradiction that Nike helps resolve is in the area of health and fitness. We all want to be fit, but it is hard to do so. It is tough to control our diet and we are too busy to actually exercise.

Nike's exhorts us to reach within ourselves and release the champion within. It tells us human stories about other champions - some famous and many not. It has done this over several years.

Now it has gone beyond that into creating a unique experience through its Fuel-band. The fuel band is a wristband that tracks every step we take and every movement that we make. It tallies this up and shows us how much fuel we have spent during the day and how it compares with our target for the day. We can share this information on social networks and compete with our friends through the Nike website.

The Nike Fuel-band is a classic word of mouth generating experience. People wear it all the time and this leads to conversation around what it is and what it does. It gives the wearer social currency. And it is true to the essence of the brand.

The Nike brand has professional marketers looking after it and ensuring that it stays true to its essence. Our next brand, the Indian Premier League, seems to blunder along on its own without a deliberate strategy and without professional brand managers. However, analysing the facets of this brand will help us understand why this brand has become so popular.

My belief is that the irrational reason for the popularity of the IPL is that we are all voyeuristic and like to know more about the lives of our stars. The IPL with its auctions, after-parties and scandals helps us see more into the lives of not just our cricket icons, but also the movie stars and business tycoons connected with the tournament.

The cultural contradiction is that while we love to watch international quality cricket, our true rivalries are often domestic. If you have ever been part of a debate around whether Mumbai is a better city or New Delhi, you know what I mean. The sporting events that generate the most passion are usually among local teams. In football, we have the local derbies - games where two teams from the same city compete. Also, club football is more avidly followed than international football. The same is true for cricket now.

The IPL is not just a sporting event. It pervades all aspects of life. It has a business angle, a social angle, a cultural angle, a human angle and so on. This is the experience of the IPL. Every year we think that the IPL will generate lesser interest than the previous year. Then some scandal or controversy erupts and the tournament becomes a talking point again. And when people talk about it, they also go and watch it and read about it.

The key point of this book is that marketing and branding is not dead, but has changed character. This chapter suggests a way to define brands that takes into account a lot of the new ideas that are floating around in the world of marketing. This is by no means definitive. This is just a suggested model that works for us, but needs to be used by more people and tested in more ways. Perhaps, it will be improved on and become more robust as time goes on. That is my fervent hope.

The Era of Experiential Marketing is Here

In his book, *What they don't teach you at Harvard Business School*, Mark McCormack talks about the time he was trying to sell sponsorship of the Wimbledon scoreboard to Rolex.

The Chairman of Rolex, Andre Heiniger, believed that he was not in the watch business but in the luxury business. As such, he thought that sponsoring of sports events was best left to watch brands like Seiko. He wasn't interested in Wimbledon.

So Mark McCormack invited Mr. Heiniger to the Royal Box at the centre court of Wimbledon as his guest to watch a match. As the Chairman of Rolex soaked in the atmosphere of Wimbledon, it dawned on him that this wasn't an ordinary sports event and the Centre Court wasn't an ordinary sports stadium. He turned to Mark McCormack and said, "This is Rolex."

That's a great example of how all the presentations and videos of Wimbledon didn't help but getting the customer to experience the product worked like magic.

Experts in the field of education believe that the best way to teach children is by letting them experience things for themselves. They stress that in order to raise self-confident children, it is important to step back and give children the opportunity to experience things for themselves. The old lecture method of teaching is now considered old hat, especially in primary schools.

All sports lovers say they would rather watch a match in a stadium than on TV. Going to the stadium involves a lot more money, a lot more time and even discomfort in terms of submitting to security checks, heavy traffic, distant parking and so on. Plus, you don't really get as close to the game as you can on TV. Yet, sports fans would rather watch the match in a stadium rather than on TV.

"It's a better experience," they say.

Experience is the most powerful selling tool there is. If a picture is worth a thousand words, then experience is worth a million at least. Especially in this new world of Prosumers.

Prosumers like to find things out for themselves. They are loyal consumers once they start to like a brand, but they hate being marketed to. The best way of communicating with Prosumers is to create opportunities for them to have great brand experiences. They will then go and share these with as many of their friends as they can.

Joseph Pine and James Gilmore created a phrase called 'Experience Economy' and wrote about it in a book of that name. The sub-title of the book is 'Work is theatre and every business a stage'. That just about sums up their prescription for how to break out of selling commodities and start selling differentiated brands.

They start off by talking about coffee. Coffee beans are traded as commodities on exchanges. If you buy coffee from there, it will end up costing you one or two cents per cup. A manufacturer could buy the beans, grind and pack them and sell the package at a grocery store. Each cup of coffee would now cost between five and ten cents. If a small diner were to buy the coffee jar, make a cup of coffee and serve it, then each cup would cost between fifty cents and a dollar.

What has happened here is that you have gone from a commodity to a product to a service. The price of coffee goes up as you ascend this ladder.

The ladder continues further. You can have the coffee in a nice coffee bar or in the restaurant of a five star hotel. The same cup of coffee now costs around five dollars. You are now paying for the experience.

There is a level even beyond experience. Pine and Gilmore talk about a friend of theirs who went to Venice and was told that the place to truly enjoy the city's atmosphere was Cafe Florian in St. Mark's Square. The friend and his wife truly enjoyed that experience and found that the coffee they had there cost them fifteen dollars per cup. They didn't mind it though; they thought they had a truly transformational experience.

According to Pine and Gilmore, products can go through five stages of evolution.

A commodity business charges for the undifferentiated product.

A goods business charges for distinctive, tangible things.

A service business charges for the activities it performs.

An experience business charges for the feelings customers get.

A transformation business charges for the change that takes place in customers by being there.

This is a nice structure to keep in mind. If the goal of the brand is to create a differentiated offering, then it must focus on climbing up this ladder towards becoming a transformational business.

As the authors argue, business is a stage and it must create memorable events for its customers, so that the memory of the experience itself becomes the product. Customers are no longer just that - they become guests.

As an aside, travellers in India must have noticed that Kingfisher Airlines referred to its passengers as guests. In the welcome video, its Chairman, Vijay Mallya, said that he had instructed the crew to treat each passenger as a "guest in my own home". Jet Airways followed this example and addresses its customers as guests, though not with as much aplomb as Kingfisher. Goes to show that it is not just about the nomenclature.

The global leader in creating brand experience is Disney. In their theme parks, the workers are called actors, the visitors are guests and the park itself is the stage. But it is not just about the theme park. Think of any brand that they create - Lion King, Toy story etc. The brand would have a movie, perhaps a TV show, a computer game, a ride and lots of merchandise. No wonder they have such loyal customers.

It's not just brands that are moving into experience. The entire economy is doing so too. In the beginning, economies were agricultural and focused on commodities. Then came the industrial revolution and the focus shifted to products produced in factories.

The industrial revolution resulted in greater income for people and a desire for a comfortable living. This meant that consumers started buying services for tasks they used to perform themselves. People eat out more often in restaurants, they hire experts from lawyers to accountants to shopping advisers to help them. We don't just buy shares, we hire investment advisers to tell us which shares to buy. We wouldn't buy a car or a computer from a company that has a poor service record.

In fact, as service becomes the dimension to compete on, it is becoming commoditized too. Take banking as an example. There was a time when banks operated only from 10am to 2 pm during weekdays and for an even shorter duration on Saturdays. Now, practically, all of them operate for eight hours a day and many are open seven days a week. All banks have ATMs and offer online banking. So these aren't differentiators either.

Similarly in the case of airlines, the ante keeps getting higher and higher. Seats that barely reclined have now become beds. Entertainment has moved to personal screens from the large screen, with an ever increasing choice of movies, TV shows, games and communication options.

However, consumer satisfaction has not really increased even though the services have become better. There are temporary spikes, but soon parity is restored by competitors, making consumers blasé about the service and taking it for granted. Brands need to keep doing more and more to stay ahead.

British Airways used to be the standard for service excellence among airlines. Sir Colin Marshall, former British Airways chairman, had stated: "What British Airways does is to go beyond the function and compete on the basis of providing an experience."

But I feel that Virgin Atlantic is more about experience than BA. Virgin offers in-flight massages, a bar where you can stand and have a drink and a lounge that is more of a clubhouse. Perhaps British Airways was about experience in an earlier era, but Virgin trumped it.

As service becomes a commodity, brands have no option but to move up to the next level. This is the experience level.

Pine and Gilmore define experience in the following way: "Experiences must provide a memorable offering that will remain with one for a long time, but in order to achieve this, the consumer - sorry, the guest, must be drawn into the offering such that they feel a sensation. And to feel the sensation, the guest must actively participate. This requires highly skilled actors who can dynamically personalise each event according to the needs, the response and the behavioural traits of the guests."

So an experience not only needs to have a stage and props, but also skilled actors who have a loose script and the ability to change it in response to their clients' desires. The experience needs to be truly interactive and the guest needs to have a great deal of control over the direction that the experience takes.

Entertainment and leisure industries are natural candidates for creating great experiences. Disney is great. McDonalds stages great birthday party experiences for their child customers. But it would be a mistake to think that brand experience is confined to any particular industry. There are several examples from other industries too.

Apple provides an experience when you enter one of its stores. The sales people there are genuine Mac fans who seem keener on having a conversation with the customer about computers and their features, than to actually sell stuff to them. The store layout (especially their flagship stores such as the one on Fifth Avenue in New York) sets the stage for the experience. The show carries on till you buy something and are ready to pay. You don't need to go to a cash counter. The sales person attending to you can swipe your card on his iTouch. He then reaches under a convenient table and miraculously pulls out the printed receipt.

Another company that apparently does a superb job of creating experiences is Progressive Corp. The company sells motor insurance and it is a matter of pride for them that they often arrive first on the scene of an accident. Their representatives do everything they can to turn a crisis into a soothing experience. They take charge, provide refreshments, arrange for the car to be towed, provide alternative transport to the passengers and, if necessary, overnight hotel accommodation. Often, they settle claims on the spot.

Clearly, experiences like the above become talking points for consumers, and especially Prosumers. This leads to positive viral effect and makes a brand strong.

Creating experiences requires new skills that companies may not have currently. To begin with, companies need to empower front office staff to a level where they can take decisions on the spot. These employees need to be actors who can respond dynamically to statements, questions and desires of their guests. This is not about a tight script such as a call centre executive might have. This is more about having a theme and then having all the actors work around that theme.

EXECUTIVE SUMMARY

So What is Marketing Unplugged?

Hello. How did you get here? Did you reach here after reading through the book from the beginning? Or did the words 'Executive Summary' draw you to the back of the book first? Either way, welcome.

If you have read the book till here, I hope it is clear that *Marketing Unplugged* is a toolkit of new techniques that you should use to come up with your marketing strategy. In this chapter, I would like to highlight the key reasons why the old way of marketing needs to change and headline the new techniques that have been detailed out in this book.

The main reason why the old marketing doesn't work now as well as before is that consumers have caught on to the old tricks. It's like a lover using the same old words for his beloved. After a while, they become routine and lose the thrill. In marketing, as in love, innovation is critical.

Consumers now know that claims made by brands are not to be relied upon. They have learnt to read the product labels more carefully and put more faith on the opinions of their friends than on the word of any brand. Consumers can even predict the tactics that brands use, and can anticipate promotional efforts of a brand.

Even if brands have a proposition that consumers would believe, it is extremely hard to reach enough number of potential customers. Gone are the days when network television provided blanket coverage. Today's fragmented media means that brand messages are also fragmented. The growth in technology allows consumers to watch their favourite TV content on multiple platforms, where they may be out of reach for advertising or where they can skip the ads.

Marketing used to bow at the altar of consumer understanding. And research was the main tool in this quest. In the early days, very few companies did consumer research. These companies had a competitive advantage. However, research has become a mature industry now and everyone is researching. Research techniques have become products that are sold to large numbers of clients. The result is that every marketer is working off the same usage and attitude study, the same insighting workshop and the same consumer clinics. No wonder that their strategies are the same.

This results in failure. Marketing is about differentiation. But if everyone is trying to differentiate in the same way, then...

'Best practices' have become the Holy Grail rather than innovation. No wonder that even major marketing giants have more failures than successes with new brands.

Overall, the picture that emerges is that the marketing function sat back and became lazy. Instead of constantly innovating, it became a process. Marketers started to enjoy the glamour of marketing and weren't prepared for the tsunami of change.

And then everything changed. Camera makers found they were competing with mobile phones. Retailers sitting on prime real estate on high street found they were competing with hole-in-the-wall players from the other end of the world. Publishers of books and music suddenly found they had to justify their existence. Businesses found that consumers wanted lots of things for free. Middlemen found themselves being squeezed out. Media persons found their content more in demand, but less remunerative than ever before.

It is in this context that we have to step back and look at marketing afresh. We need to forget that marketing is a process and take an unplugged view of it.

In this book, we have spoken of experts who tell us that it is better to observe behaviour than to ask questions in research. This startlingly simple credo has been forgotten in the excitement of projective techniques and ever more sophisticated data analysis.

When we find patterns in consumer behaviour, we have to look for deep reasons to explain these patterns. Marketers have a tendency to look for rational explanations. But often, the real reason why people buy something has to do with some deep cultural or irrational factors. Irrational itself is a bad word. Perhaps, instinctive would be better.

A whole school of economics has sprung up that combines the above into a new field of study called Behavioural Economics. Experts in this new field offer seemingly better insights into consumer behaviour than conventional research techniques.

Experts have also been looking at the very nature of brands and questioning why they exist. One of their findings is that the contact that brands have

Suman Srivastava

with consumers needs to change. In the past, the contact was one on one, brand with consumer. Today, it is more complex and brands are expected to play a role in society. Brands need to have a larger purpose. Some brands have started defining their purpose and work towards fulfilling it. These are currently more successful than brands that have not.

Brands have also been experimenting with how to communicate with the new consumer who is smarter than ever before. The education system realised long ago that children learn better through experiences rather than through structured lessons. Now brands have begun to do that too. Create experiences for consumers that make them realise what the brand is all about rather than just tell them.

There are several other ideas that experts have come up with. I have tried to combine some of those ideas into a new narrative that I have decided to call *Marketing Unplugged*. This narrative offers no guarantees for success. All it does is goad you onto a path of constant innovation, which, I believe, will increase the chances of success.

For the rest, pray!

END OF BOOK

BIBLIOGRAPHY

Anderson, Chris. Free: *The Future of a Radical Price*. New York: Hyperion, 2009. Print.

Anderson, Chris. *The Long Tail: Why the Future of Business Is Selling Less of More*. New York: Hyperion, 2006. Print.

Ariely, Dan. *Predictably Irrational: The Hidden Forces That Shape Our Decisions*. New York, NY: HarperCollins, 2008. Print.

Asimov, Isaac. *The Tragedy of the Moon*. London: Abelard-Schuman, 1974. Print.

Dixit, Avinash K., and Barry Nalebuff. *The Art of Strategy: A Game Theorist's Guide to Success in Business & Life*. Print.

Ghemawat, Pankaj. *World 3.0: Global Prosperity and How to Achieve It*. Boston, MA: Harvard

Business Review, 2011. Print.

Gladwell, Malcolm. *The Tipping Point: How Little Things Can Make a Big Difference*. Boston: Little, Brown, 2000. Print.

Guha, Ramachandra. *A Corner of a Foreign Field: The Indian History of a British Sport*. London: Picador, 2002. Print.

Iyengar, Sheena. *The Art of Choosing*. New York: Twelve, 2010. Print.

Jackson, Daniel M., and Paul Fulberg. *Sonic Branding: An Introduction*. London: Palgrave Macmillan, 2003. Print.

Kim, W. Chan., and Renée Mauborgne. *Blue Ocean Strategy: How to Create Uncontested Market Space and Make the Competition Irrelevant*. Boston, MA: Harvard Business School, 2005. Print.

Lindström, Martin. *Buyology: How Everything We Believe about Why We Buy Is Wrong*. London: Random House Business, 2008. Print.

McCormack, Mark H. *What They Don't Teach You at Harvard Business School*. Toronto: Bantam, 1984. Print.

Morgan, Adam. *Eating the Big Fish: How Challenger Brands Can Compete against Brand Leaders*. New York: John Wiley, 1999. Print.

Packard, Vance. *The Hidden Persuaders*. New York: Pocket, 1962. Print.

Pine, B. Joseph., and James H. Gilmore. *The Experience Economy: Work Is Theatre & Every Business a Stage*. Boston: Harvard Business School, 1999. Print.

Rapaille, Clotaire. *The Culture Code: An Ingenious Way to Understand Why People around the World Buy and Live as They Do*. New York: Broadway, 2006. Print.

Sun, TZU, and S. B. Griffths. *The Art of War*. *Place of Publication Not Identified*: Oxford U, 1971. Print.

Taleb, Nassim Nicholas. *The Black Swan: The Impact of the Highly Improbable*. New York: Random House, 2007. Print.

Tofler, Alvin. *The Third Wave*. New York: Morrow, 1980. Print.

Underhill, Paco. *Why We Buy: The Science of Shopping*. New York: Simon & Schuster, 1999. Print.

Varma, Pavan K. *Being Indian: The Truth about Why the Twenty-first Century Will Be India's*. New Delhi: Viking, 2004. Print.

Wilcox, Matthew. *The Business of Choice: Marketing to Consumers' Instincts*. Print.

ABOUT THE AUTHOR

Suman Srivastava enjoys doing new things. A graduate of Delhi University, IIM Ahmedabad and IMD Lausanne, he is an advertising man, strategist, author, marathon runner, teacher, social worker, sports fan, creative bartender and an entrepreneur.

Suman started his career with Lintas and was part of the team that set up SSC & B. He moved on to Euro RSCG and later became its CEO, and also acted as the Chief Strategy Officer for Euro RSCG, Asia Pacific.

He has also acted as the Chairman of Euro RSCG's emerging markets planning council and was a member of its global management committee.

Suman loves startups. He was part of the team that started SSC & B Lintas and later part of the team that started Euro RSCG India. He has a track record of changing jobs only in the years when India has hosted the cricket world cup. He got his first job in 1987, his second in 1996 and his third (Marketing Unplugged) in 2011.

Marketing Unplugged is an innovation firm started by Suman, focusing on helping Indian companies create marketing innovations to achieve extraordinary growth. In this capacity, he is associated with brands such as Raymond (suitings), Carat Lane (online jewellery), Network18 (media), Sweekar (cooking oil), Spuul (entertainment app), Johnson & Johnson (OTC), Navneet (stationery) to name a few. He also oversees the strategic planning function at FCB Ulka.

Suman believes that he was put on earth to be a teacher. He loves teaching and has done sessions at IIMs in Ahmedabad and Bangalore, ISB Hyderabad, IITs at Bombay and Kharagpur, MICA and several other management institutes across the country. He has also run workshops for clients like Microsoft, Intel, Reckitt Benckiser, Max New York Life, Dainik Bhaskar and Bharat Petroleum.

Brand building is a passion for Suman. He has been closely associated with brands from India's leading companies including Hindustan Unilever, Reckitt Benckiser, Intel, Microsoft, IBM, Dell, HDFC Bank, Bharat Petroleum, Reliance, Mahindra & Mahindra, Bajaj Auto and Philips.

He is active in the voluntary sector where he works for causes that range from schooling for slum children to child sexual abuse to rural tourism to getting India to 'Give' more. He is a trustee of two NGOs, an adviser to a third and volunteers with several others.

Suman has run the half marathon three times and loves to make creative cocktails.

www.ingramcontent.com/pod-product-compliance
Lightning Source LLC
Chambersburg PA
CBHW011159220326
41597CB00026BA/4671